CONVECTION OVEN COOKING
made simple

CONVECTION OVEN COOKING
made simple

A Guide and Cookbook to Get the Most Out of Your Convection Oven

Janet A. Zimmerman
Photography by Marija Vidal

ROCKRIDGE PRESS

For general information on our other products and services or to obtain technical support, please contact our Customer Care Department within the United States at (866) 744-2665, or outside the United States at (510) 253-0500.

Rockridge Press publishes its books in a variety of electronic and print formats. Some content that appears in print may not be available in electronic books, and vice versa.

Interior and Cover Designer: Linda Snorina
Art Producer: Karen Williams
Editor: Van Van Cleave
Production Manager: Michael Kay
Production Editor: Melissa Edeburn
Photography © Marija Vidal, 2020.
Food styling by Elisabet Der Nederlanden.
Author photo © Court Mast.
Cover image: Crispy Garlic Chicken Thighs with Potatoes and Carrots, page 68.

ISBN: Print 978-1-64739-053-2 | eBook 978-1-64739-054-9

R0

to Dave,

who gladly helps me develop recipes,
eats whatever dishes I need to test,
listens to me rant, and washes dishes.

SPICY MEXICAN-STYLE CROSTINI page 38

Contents

INTRODUCTION

The history of kitchen appliances is full of promises to make cooking faster, easier, or both. Microwave ovens, slow cookers, electric pressure cookers, air fryers, and multicookers have provided the home cook with so many options that they appear to have left the traditional kitchen range and oven behind.

Don't get me wrong—I think these appliances can be a great addition to the kitchen (I'd better think that; I've written books on both pressure cookers and multicookers). What surprises me, though, are those cooks who seem to have sworn off conventional cooking methods—"I never use my oven anymore," they claim with glee, as if oven cooking is the worst idea in the world. This attitude makes me sad.

On the other hand, in a way, I get it. I've lived much of my life in rental apartments, many of which had, shall we say, less-than-perfect ovens. It's tough to do serious cooking in an oven that can't hold a steady temperature or that takes forever to heat up. (Don't even ask me about the gas oven with the broiler element in a bottom "drawer," which I could use only if I lay down on the floor and tossed food inside it.)

It was a less-than-perfect oven that inspired me to buy an early countertop convection oven. Before that time, the only available small ovens were marketed as toaster ovens—in my experience, good at neither toasting nor baking. But the oven I bought was outstanding. It was perfect for cooking for one or two, as I usually did, and it heated up quickly and held its temperature.

Best of all, it was a convection oven. I'd never used one before, and I fell in love. It heated fast, and it cooked fast. It produced fabulous crusts on pizzas and pies, it roasted vegetables perfectly, and it even broiled fish.

Lest you think my love of convection ovens is due simply to that countertop marvel, I skip ahead to my introduction to full-size convection ovens. Two things happened: I started teaching in a kitchen with convection ovens, and I moved in with Dave, the love of my life and owner of a convection oven (no connection, I swear). As I became accustomed to convection ovens, I grew to appreciate their dependably even heat and quicker cook times, to the point that I now rarely cook with conventional oven heat.

It's true that both countertop and full-size convection ovens involve a learning curve. I'm lucky to have avoided any full-blown disasters, but I have had a few recipes turn out "nicely browned" (in my family, that's Mom-speak for "all but burned"). Over the years, though, I've learned the ins and outs of convection ovens and now, cooking with them is second nature to me.

That's why I jumped at the chance to write this book—I wanted to make convection cooking as easy for you as I know it can be. So many home cooks are intimidated by their convection ovens, but I want you to know that with a little practice, you can grow to love yours as much as I love mine.

ROASTED DUCK BREASTS WITH OVEN FRIES page 82

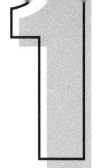

CONVECTION COOKING WITH EASE

I've taught cooking classes for years, and I can't count the number of students who tell me that they have a convection setting on their oven but are scared to use it. I'm here to tell you, if you can use an oven, you can use a convection oven. Yes, it's true that professional bakers use them, but you don't have to be a pro to get the most from convection. Keep reading to find out exactly how easy it is, and you'll become fast friends with your convection oven. Who knows? You may even start to feel like a pro.

COOKING WITH CONVECTION

Once upon a time, convection ovens were huge, industrial-size appliances used exclusively in professional bakeries. Pans and pans of croissants or tarts were loaded onto multiple racks in the cooking chamber; a separate section contained a powerful heating element and a fan that blew precisely heated air into the box to surround the pastries. Those giants are still around, but smaller home models of convection ovens have found their way into kitchens across the country and around the world. Their efficiency, even heat, and deliciously reliable results have created a boom in popularity.

How the Convection Oven Works

In the most basic terms, convection is simply the motion of air (or liquid) as it heats and cools. As you might remember from science class, warmer air has faster-moving molecules than cold air, which makes it less dense. The warm air thus expands and rises, while the cooler air sinks. Heat is transferred to the colder air, until the temperature levels out. This "natural" convection is evident everywhere—think of the uniform heating of food in a saucepan, the way the temperature in a heated room evens out, or weather patterns. Conventional ovens rely on a combination of this natural process together with radiant heat.

The convection in a convection oven, on the other hand, is what is called "forced" convection. That just means that it results from a fan (or a pump, in the case of liquid) that speeds up the natural process. The hot air blowing through a convection oven makes the effective temperature higher—much as how wind chill reduces the effective temperature on cold winter days.

Seven Reasons to Cook with Convection

1. **Faster preheating.** The fan, especially if it's set with a third heating element, will heat the oven up to 25 percent faster than a conventional oven. In a small countertop oven, the difference is even more noticeable.

2. **Quicker cooking time.** In a convection oven, heat is transferred to the food faster, which results in cooking times up to 30 percent shorter than in conventional ovens.

3. **Greater energy efficiency.** The faster preheat and cooking times mean that your oven will be on for less time, saving energy and keeping your kitchen a bit cooler.

4. **More even cooking.** The convection fan helps eliminate hot and cold spots in your oven. That translates to batches of perfect cookies, whether you're cooking one batch or two at a time, often without having to rotate the pans.

5. **Better browning.** The hot air circulating around your food will not only cook it more evenly, but also will produce beautiful browning. Picture crisp, golden chicken skin, a lovely bread crumb topping on your macaroni and cheese, and a perfect crust on your beef roast.

6. **Flakier crusts and pastries.** The higher effective temperature in your oven virtually guarantees better piecrusts, croissants, and pastries. These doughs get their light, flaky texture when the butter between the layers melts, releasing steam and creating air pockets. The faster that happens, the bigger the air pockets, and the flakier the pastry.

7. **Crispiness without frying.** With a few tips, you can "oven-fry" foods with very little added oil, whether shoestring sweet potatoes or chicken nuggets. Much like dedicated air fryers, convection ovens can produce lower-fat versions of traditional fried foods—without sacrificing any of the crunch factor.

CONVECTION COOKING MADE SIMPLE

With very few exceptions, you can cook anything with convection that you do conventionally. In some cases, you won't notice a difference, except for faster preheating and slightly faster cooking. In others, you'll get noticeably better results with only minor tweaks to your recipes.

In this section, I'll go over everything you need to know to approach your convection oven with confidence. With a review of the differences between full-size and countertop models, an explanation of the various convection settings, and suggestions for helpful tools and cookware, you'll learn all you need to start on the many recipes that use this revolutionary kitchen appliance. You'll even find out how to adapt your own favorite recipes with certain success.

Size Considerations

All the recipes in this book can be made in either a full-size or countertop convection oven, although a smaller oven may necessitate cooking in batches or making other minor changes. I'll explain any required adjustments in the recipes themselves.

FULL-SIZE

Full-size convection ovens (or ovens with convection settings) fall into one of two broad categories. "True convection" ovens (also called "European convection" ovens) have three heating elements. As with conventional ovens, one is positioned at the top and one at the bottom. The third is in the back, along with the fan, which blows heated air into the oven.

The other style of convection oven, which doesn't really have its own name, has only the top and bottom heating elements, so the fan circulates air that's heated by those elements. In theory, "true convection" ovens are supposed to provide better results, with fewer hot and cold spots. In practice, the other type can be quite effective. I've known professional chefs who consider them virtually indistinguishable.

One thing to keep in mind is that gas convection ovens, while they exist, have never quite gotten it right. If you want a gas stovetop and don't have room for a wall oven, look to dual-fuel ranges, which combine gas burners with an electric oven.

COUNTERTOP

Countertop convection ovens come in several sizes and configurations, but most of the popular models are large enough to hold a 9-by-13-inch pan, with enough vertical space for cakes and bread loaves or a small turkey breast. Some are taller, with two racks that can be used for two baking sheets or cake layers at a time. Others have a curved interior section at the back to accommodate a larger round pan for pies or pizzas. They're great as a backup oven for holiday cooking or entertaining and can be ideal for couples or small families. They can also be a lifesaver during hot summers, when you probably don't want to heat a full-size oven.

Rack Placement

Since convection ovens heat very evenly, rack placement isn't nearly as crucial as with a conventional oven. That said, there are a few instances when it does make a difference:

- If you're cooking two sheets of cookies, or meat on one pan and potatoes on another, you'll want to position the racks evenly; neither one too close to the top or bottom elements. Even spacing will mean even air flow, and thus more even cooking.

- In smaller ovens, use the lowest rack slot when cooking large items such as turkey breasts or rib roasts to ensure enough space over the top of the food for the hot air to circulate.

- If you're using the broiler, you'll want to position the rack close to the broiler, which is usually in the top position.

When rack placement is integral to a recipe in this book, I'll always tell you how to position them.

The countertop model also provides a less expensive opportunity to test out convection cooking, if you're undecided about whether to invest in a full-size convection range. Keep in mind, though, that while a few high-end countertop models are available with "true convection," they tend to be very expensive; most common models do not have a separate heating element/fan combination.

Settings and Features

I'm old enough to remember when ovens had two settings: bake and broil. You could change the temperature on the bake setting, and that was the limit of your control. Today's convection ovens are a wonderfully different story. Both full-size and countertop convection ovens offer a wide variety of settings. Some will even allow you to turn off the convection setting and revert to conventional oven mode. Once you get the hang of the different settings, you'll learn which setting will give you the best results. Of course, in my recipes, I will tell you the best settings, so keep reading and you'll learn even faster.

Convection Roast. In culinary terms, "roasting" is generally used to describe cooking meats and vegetables without any sauces. Generally, high temperatures are used, except for when you're slow roasting (as for fish), in which case the temperature will be significantly lower. On most ovens, the Convection Roast setting just means that both the top and bottom elements will be on while pre-heating. In some ovens, both elements will cycle on and off to keep the oven at the desired temperature; in others, only the bottom element will stay on after the oven is preheated.

Convection Bake. When professional cooks talk about "baking," they usually mean cooking batters and doughs to make baked goods. Baking usually calls for lower temperatures than roasting. Most convection ovens employ only the bottom element on the Convection Bake setting. It will cycle on and off as necessary to keep the oven at the correct temperature.

Convection Broil. Like a conventional broiler, the Convection Broil setting will use only the top element, which will remain on during the entire cooking process. Some ovens have both low and high broiler settings. The broiler is handy when you want to brown or blacken the top of something, such as the crumbs on a gratin or the skin of red peppers so they can be peeled.

Convection Fry. Some countertop convection ovens double as air fryers, which are really just small, powerful convection ovens with a basket to increase air flow. Most of these models use a faster fan setting and higher temperatures for more drying out and thus browning of the outsides of foods like oven fries or chicken wings. Generally, these settings use both heating elements.

Convection Toast. Most countertop ovens can also double as toasters and have a setting for toast and, usually, one for bagels. You can choose a variety of dark or light toast settings and sometimes specify the number of slices. Both elements will heat up (the bagel setting will set one element hotter than the other to toast the cut side of each half while only warming the exterior).

STEPS FOR SUCCESSFUL CONVECTION COOKING

So, now you know how easy a convection oven is to use and how it will improve your life, or at least your cooking. There are a few steps you can take to ensure you get the absolute best results from your convection oven:

Read the manual. I know, everyone hates manuals. But every oven is different, and I can't tell you all the details that your manual can. You don't have to read all the fine print, but most manuals will give you the important stuff up front, and I recommend that you at least read that section.

Test your oven. Not all oven brands and models perform exactly the same. I strongly recommend you invest in an oven thermometer and spend one Sunday afternoon measuring temperatures. You'll get better results, and you'll get cool-geek bragging rights. I suggest testing three settings. 300°F or 325°F, 350°F or 375°F, and 450°F or 500°F. You may find, especially if you're using a countertop oven, that the oven will signal that's it at the set temperature 5 to 10 minutes before it actually reaches that temperature, so wait to measure. Then, when you cook, you can have your oven's actual temperatures in mind and make the necessary adjustments.

Preheat your oven. If your oven isn't fully heated when you place your food inside, the cooking time will be affected. While cooking a dish for a few extra minutes to make up the difference isn't usually the end of the world, I recommend giving yourself the best starting point as you begin to use your oven. In some cases—as with pastry, for instance—you'll get better results if the oven is fully heated before you start cooking.

Test your food early. Even the best recipes can't take into account all the different ovens that readers use. And even if we recipe writers could do that, we can't account for natural differences in ingredients. For instance, the moisture level in your potatoes can cause them to cook at a different rate than my potatoes. Your chicken thighs might be larger, or colder, than mine. Likewise, the construction of your baking pans can affect the cooking time. For these reasons, I always set a timer for three-quarters of the way through the total cooking time to check my food, even when I've made a recipe before.

Conserve heat. Even though you need to check on your food, try not to open the oven door more than necessary. A convection oven usually maintains its heat level better than a conventional oven, but you still don't want that heat to escape. If possible, turn on the light and do a visual check (with cookies or casserole toppings, for instance). If you need to check your food's temperature or texture, open the oven, remove the dish, and close the door before testing. If you leave the door open while you insert your cake tester, for example, the temperature is likely to plummet.

CONVECTION-FRIENDLY COOKWARE

Cooking with a convection oven doesn't require special cookware or accessories, since any materials that are safe for a conventional oven can be used in a convection oven. That said, it can be even easier and more fun if you have a few specific tools in your kitchen. You probably have many of these already, and the rest are inexpensive and easy to find.

Pots and pans. It's great to have cooking vessels in a wide variety of sizes and shapes, but I'll share the ones I use most often in this book's recipes. First, you'll want a 9-by-13-inch ceramic, stoneware, metal, or tempered glass baking dish. For a countertop oven, look for a pan without handles or with handles that rise straight up (rather than out) so it will be sure to fit. Other recipes call for a 9-inch square baking pan or a 9-inch tart pan. I also use muffin tins for a couple of recipes; a tin with 6 muffins will fit in a countertop oven (you can either halve the recipe or cook in batches). A 5- to 6-quart Dutch oven is great for recipes that start on the stove and end in the oven. I also often call for a 10-inch cast-iron skillet for recipes that use both the oven and stovetop. You can use any oven-safe heavy skillet or sauté pan, but avoid shallow pans or those with steeply sloped sides; they don't hold as much food. And finally, you might want to have a loaf pan for quick breads and a roasting pan for a large roast or whole turkey.

Sheet pans and racks. If there's one item I can't be without, it's the sheet pan (a.k.a. rimmed baking sheet). A half-sheet pan (about 13 by 18 inches) is ideal for a full-size oven, while a quarter-sheet pan will fit inside most countertop models. You'll often find sheet pans sold with racks that fit inside them. These racks can be used for cooling, but they're also great for cooking—they lift foods up off the pan for better air circulation, which gets foods browner and crisper.

Meat and oven thermometers. It's wise to invest in an oven thermometer to make sure your oven is as hot as it thinks it is (see page 7). And to ensure safe meat temperatures, you'll also want an instant-read meat thermometer. One with a probe that's attached to a base unit outside the oven is handy for large roasts and whole poultry, but not essential.

Silicone baking mats. Silicone mats will protect your sheet pans and keep foods from sticking. (I love parchment paper, but it tends to blow around when the convection fan is on, so I usually reserve it for things like lining cake pans and wrapping salmon packets.) The mats come in the same size as half- and quarter-sheet pans, so you can get a mat for every size.

Pizza stone or steel. A pizza stone or, even better, a pizza steel will make awesome pizza. That said, I own neither. Pizza steels are very expensive, and pizza stones are heavy, fragile, and bulky, and I just don't make that much pizza. If you do, or you want a new hobby, they can be a wonderful investment.

Other equipment. Heavy oven mitts or potholders are essential for handling hot items, and if your counters aren't heat-proof, you'll want a large trivet or cutting board to hold hot pans after cooking. Long-handled tongs are great for tossing vegetables and transferring foods from pots to cutting boards.

CONVERTING AND ADAPTING RECIPES FOR THE CONVECTION OVEN

After you've made all the recipes in this book—or, likely, even sooner—you may start wondering how to convert your existing baking and roasting recipes for convection cooking. Unfortunately, there's no magic formula for the process. It'll take some experimentation. The good news is this: I can give you some starting points, and with care and attention, you'll be able to make delicious food even the first time trying.

In most cases, baking recipes take more tinkering than roasting recipes, so you'll want to exercise more caution with a loaf of bread than with roasted potatoes. The smaller the food item, the more crucial time and temperature

What Not to Convection Cook

While your convection oven will probably become one of your favorite kitchen appliances, it's not ideal for cooking everything. Even expert bakers disagree on some foods—one cookbook author raves about pound cake baked on the convection setting, while another advises against it. However, all will tell you to avoid using the convection settings for delicate foods, such as the following:

- **Soufflés:** The whole point of a soufflé is its light, airy texture, and that's difficult to achieve with the convection fan on. The air movement can cause uneven rising, resulting in a sad, misshapen soufflé.

- **Custards:** The hot blowing air of a convection setting may cause the top of a custard mixture to cook too fast and dry out before the center is set. In the worst case, you'll end up with a cracked top.

- **Angel food and chiffon cakes:** As with soufflés, these cakes need to rise evenly. Moving air can distort their shape.

will be—naturally, a cookie will overbake way faster than a cake, and a steak will overcook before a whole chicken. On the plus side, if you're baking cookies or small appetizers, you can test one or two, so if you don't get it exactly right, you still have the rest of the batch to achieve perfection.

As you start converting recipes, it'll be easier if you reduce only the time or the temperature, not both. I usually start with the time. As you become more familiar with your convection settings, you can start to adjust both in small increments. Many experts recommend reducing the time and leaving the temperature constant when roasting vegetables and meats, and reversing that for baking.

Conversely, these recipes can generally be made in a conventional oven as well. You could do one of two things: Set the oven to a little higher temperature and go for the same baking time (although check early), or keep the temperature the same and cook it for longer. Keep a watchful eye to make sure the top is browning evenly, and rotate the pan if necessary. All ovens are different, so you'll soon figure out what works best in yours.

Oh, and be sure to keep a notebook handy and write down what works and what doesn't, so you'll remember for the next time!

Time

If you're keeping the temperature the same with your recipe, you can start by reducing the cooking time by about 30 percent for convection cooking. Check your food and see if it's done the way the recipe indicates it should be. In most cases, you'll see a reduction of somewhere between 20 and 30 percent of the called-for cooking time, but it might be as little as 10 percent.

Temperature

Most experts suggest reducing the temperature by 25 degrees when converting a recipe from conventional to convection cooking. That's never really made sense to me, though. Here's what I think: Lots of baking recipes call for a cooking temperature of 350°F, and in that case, switching to 325°F for convection cooking works pretty well. But it's not going to translate to other starting temperatures—25 degrees is a smaller percentage of 400 degrees than it is of 350, and a larger percentage of 300, if that's your starting temperature. (Okay, so I'm a geek.) You can try reducing the temperature by a straight 25 degrees, but you'll do better to reduce it by about 7 percent, if you can stand to do the math.

You still should start checking your food about three-quarters of the way through the cooking time, just to be on the safe side.

THE RECIPES

The recipes in this book are divided by the meal or course, such as Breakfast and Brunch; Vegetables, Sides, and Appetizers; and Desserts and Sweets. The three chapters devoted to entrées are subdivided by main ingredient or type: Seafood; Poultry; and Beef, Pork, and Lamb. All the recipes are flagged with handy labels—Dairy-Free, Gluten-Free, Vegetarian, Vegan, One-Pan, and Under 30 Minutes—so you can easily choose meals that meet your dietary requirements and cooking style.

At the beginning of each recipe, I list the prep time, cooking time, and total time. A few recipes benefit from extra time for things like chilling dough or marinating meat, but when these steps are not absolutely necessary, those times are not included in the total.

I've tried to be as accurate as possible, but as I've mentioned, ovens vary, and cooking times are also affected by factors such as the size, temperature, or age of ingredients. I'll always include information about, for instance, the desired internal temperatures of meats and how the finished dish should look; you can use these "doneness cues" as a guide in addition to cooking times.

Each recipe begins with a short introduction, called a headnote in cookbook lingo. You may be tempted to skip reading these, but I often include important information about the ingredients or instructions here.

Each recipe is followed by one or more tips, which may include suggestions for ingredient substitutions or variations, time-saving ideas, or creative uses for leftovers. This is also where you'll find any adaptations necessary if you're using a smaller countertop oven.

As much as possible, I've chosen recipes that are fast and fairly simple to make. (Some of the breads and desserts are more involved, and there are a few "special occasion" recipes included.) Generally, they call for fewer than 10 ingredients, all of which can be found in most grocery stores. Finally, I've tried to include a mix of different styles and cuisines in the book, so I hope you'll find a variety of dishes that appeal to you.

Notes about Ingredients

I call for a few specific ingredients repeatedly throughout the book. Here's what you need to know about them.

Salt. I used Diamond Crystal kosher salt when developing these recipes. If you're using fine (table or sea) salt, use half as much.

Butter. I call for unsalted butter in my recipes, but if you don't have it, you can use salted. You may want to reduce or eliminate the salt called for, especially in desserts and breakfast sweets.

Broth. My recipes generally call for low-sodium broths. If you have the regular varieties, just reduce the salt in the recipe. You can always add more salt after cooking, but you can't take it out.

Parmesan cheese. I use a lot of "Parm" in my savory recipes. If you can afford it, traditional Parmigiano-Reggiano from Italy is wonderful, but it's not necessary. There are several good domestic versions on the market;

SarVecchio from Sartori is one of my favorites, and Trader Joe's has its own very good version. Please avoid pre-grated versions, especially the dreaded green can. They don't taste the same, and many contain anti-clumping agents that can prevent them from melting well.

Vegetable oil. I generally use a mild vegetable oil or regular (that is, not extra-virgin) olive oil in my recipes. You can substitute any refined oil you like, but avoid anything with a very low smoke point. When I do call for extra-virgin olive oil, it's for the flavor, so I don't recommend you substitute.

Panko bread crumbs. Panko bread crumbs are specially made for coating foods to be fried or baked, or topping casseroles for an extra crunchy layer. Try to find a Japanese brand; they tend to be flakier rather than pebbly. Gluten-free panko is also available.

Now, let's cook!

DUTCH BABY WITH MIXED BERRIES page 19

2

BREAKFAST
AND BRUNCH

CINNAMON-APPLE GRANOLA

DAIRY-FREE | GLUTEN-FREE | VEGETARIAN | VEGAN OPTION | UNDER 30 MINUTES

Making your own granola is so easy and delicious, you might never buy it again, and the convection oven produces crunchy, golden brown clusters of oats and nuts. Spread the oats carefully—if you leave them in small clumps rather than separating them out completely, you'll get a better texture.

SERVES 6

Prep Time: 5 minutes

Cook Time: 15 minutes

3 cups gluten-free old-fashioned rolled oats

1 cup slivered almonds

1 cup unsweetened coconut chips

½ cup honey or pure maple syrup

⅓ cup packed light brown sugar

¼ cup vegetable oil

1 teaspoon ground cinnamon

¼ teaspoon kosher salt

2 cups chopped dried apples

1. Select Convection Bake and preheat the oven to 325°F.

2. In a large bowl, combine the oats, almonds, coconut, honey, brown sugar, oil, cinnamon, and salt and mix well. Spread the mixture in an even layer on a sheet pan.

3. Bake for 6 minutes. Remove the pan and stir the granola. Return to the oven and continue baking until the nuts and oats are golden brown and crisp, another 6 to 8 minutes.

4. Let cool, then stir in the apples.

FOR COUNTERTOP OVENS: Use a smaller sheet pan. Bake the granola in two batches if you like it really crunchy, or just stir it several times while it bakes.

SIMPLE SWAP: Instead of dried apples and almonds, you can substitute whatever dried fruits and nuts you like.

SAVE FOR LATER: Store leftovers in an airtight container for up to 5 days.

CRANBERRY-ORANGE MUFFINS

VEGETARIAN

I got the unusual mixing method for these muffins from Stella Parks, baker extraordinaire and author of BraveTart. *Mixing the dry ingredients with the butter coats the flour and keeps gluten formation to a minimum, resulting in a tender crumb.*

SERVES 12

Prep Time: 15 minutes

Cook Time: 25 minutes

Nonstick cooking spray

2¼ cups all-purpose flour

¾ cup sugar

2 teaspoons baking powder

Finely grated zest and juice of 1 orange (about 2 teaspoons zest and ¼ cup juice)

½ teaspoon kosher salt

¼ teaspoon baking soda

10 tablespoons (1¼ sticks) unsalted butter, at room temperature, cut into ½-inch pieces

¼ cup whole milk

2 large eggs

1 teaspoon vanilla extract

1 cup dried cranberries

1. Select Convection Bake and preheat the oven to 350°F. Coat a 12-cup muffin tin with cooking spray.

2. Combine the flour, sugar, baking powder, orange zest, salt, baking soda, and butter in the bowl of a stand mixer with a paddle attachment (or use a hand mixer). Mix on low speed for about 2 minutes, until the butter has broken into very small clumps. The mixture will look powdery but hold together when pinched.

3. Add the milk, orange juice, eggs, and vanilla. Mix on low just until combined and very thick.

4. Stir in the cranberries.

5. Divide the batter evenly among the prepared muffin cups. Bake until the muffins are puffed, golden brown, and firm to the touch, about 25 minutes, rotating the tin after 15 minutes if cooking unevenly.

FOR COUNTERTOP OVENS: Use a 6-cup muffin tin and bake in two batches.

SIMPLE SWAP: Try fresh or frozen blueberries instead of cranberries. Or you can leave out the cranberries and orange, double the milk, and add 1 teaspoon of ground cinnamon and 1 cup of finely chopped apples.

SAUSAGE-CHEDDAR SCONES

UNDER 30 MINUTES

These savory scones filled with sharp Cheddar cheese, scallions, and sausage make a delicious, portable breakfast.

SERVES 6

Prep Time: 15 minutes

Cook Time: 15 minutes

1½ cups all-purpose flour

2 teaspoons baking powder

½ teaspoon kosher salt

3 tablespoons unsalted butter, very cold

1 cup coarsely grated sharp Cheddar cheese

2 or 3 scallions, finely chopped (about ¼ cup)

8 ounces breakfast sausage, cooked and coarsely chopped

1 large egg, beaten, divided

½ cup heavy (whipping) cream

1. Select Convection Bake and preheat the oven to 425°F. Line a sheet pan with a silicone baking mat.

2. In a large bowl, whisk together the flour, baking powder, and salt. Using the large holes of a cheese grater, grate the butter into the flour mixture and stir to combine. Mix in the cheese, scallions, and sausage.

3. Pour 1 tablespoon of the beaten egg into a small bowl and set aside. Whisk the cream into the remaining egg. Add the egg mixture to the flour and butter mixture. The dough should hold together but be shaggy rather than moist.

4. Transfer the dough to a lightly floured work surface. Gather it together into a rectangle. Fold the dough into thirds and press together. Repeat.

5. Form the dough into a smooth 6-inch disk. Cut the disk into 6 wedges, and carefully transfer them to the prepared pan.

6. Brush the scones with the reserved egg.

7. Bake for 15 to 18 minutes, until golden brown, rotating halfway through if they're browning unevenly. Cool on the pan for about 10 minutes. Serve warm or at room temperature.

SIMPLE SWAP: Swap the Cheddar for another strongly flavored cheese, such as Gruyère, and crumbled cooked bacon for the sausage.

DUTCH BABY WITH MIXED BERRIES

VEGETARIAN | UNDER 30 MINUTES

A Dutch baby, or Finnish pancake, is sort of like a giant, mildly sweet popover. Rich and eggy, it puffs up beautifully in the oven. Sadly, it will sink a bit as you cut into it, but don't worry. It's still impressive.

SERVES 4

Prep Time: 10 minutes

Cook Time: 20 minutes

3 tablespoons unsalted butter, at room temperature

¾ cup whole milk

3 large eggs

½ cup all-purpose flour

¼ cup sugar, plus 2 tablespoons

½ teaspoon vanilla extract

¼ teaspoon kosher salt

1 (10- to 12-ounce) package frozen mixed berries, thawed

1 tablespoon freshly squeezed lemon juice

1. Select Convection Roast and preheat the oven to 425°F. Put the butter in a 10-inch cast-iron skillet and place it in the oven while the oven heats.

2. Meanwhile, make the batter. In a blender (or in a large bowl with a hand mixer), combine the milk, eggs, flour, the 2 tablespoons of sugar, vanilla, and salt and blend until smooth.

3. When the oven is at temperature and the butter in the skillet has stopped foaming, remove the skillet from the oven and pour in the batter.

4. Turn the oven to Convection Bake and reduce the temperature to 400°F. Bake for 20 minutes without opening the oven. The pancake should be puffed and golden brown, with darker brown edges. Bake for another 5 minutes if necessary.

5. Meanwhile, pour the berries and their juices into a small bowl. Add the remaining ¼ cup of sugar and the lemon juice, and stir to dissolve the sugar.

6. When the pancake is done, slice into wedges and serve with a scoop of berries on top.

SIMPLE SWAP: Instead of using berries, drizzle the top of the baked pancake with lemon juice and sprinkle with confectioners' sugar.

HAM AND CHEESE PASTRIES

UNDER 30 MINUTES

These pastries are easy to prepare because they are made with store-bought puff pastry. If possible, use puff pastry made with all butter (I recommend Dufour brand).

SERVES 4

Prep Time: 10 minutes

Cook Time: 20 minutes

¾ cup diced ham

½ cup shredded Gruyère or other Swiss-style cheese

2 tablespoons cream cheese, softened

1 tablespoon Dijon mustard

1 sheet frozen puff pastry, thawed

1 large egg, beaten

2 tablespoons finely grated Parmesan cheese

SAVE FOR LATER: Construct these up to step 5 (omit the egg wash) and then freeze for baking later. Let thaw overnight, then continue with the recipe as directed.

SIMPLE SWAP: Instead of puff pastry, you can use homemade or store-bought pie dough. Cut into large rounds and form half-moon-shaped pastries.

1. Select Convection Bake and preheat the oven to 350°F. Line a sheet pan with a silicone baking mat.

2. In a medium bowl, stir together the ham, shredded cheese, cream cheese, and mustard.

3. Lightly flour a cutting board. Unfold the puff pastry sheet onto the board. Using a rolling pin, gently roll the dough to smooth out the folds, sealing any tears. Cut the dough into four squares.

4. Scoop a quarter of the ham mixture into the center of each puff pastry square and spread it evenly in a triangle shape over half the pastry, leaving a ½-inch border around the edges. Fold the pastry diagonally over the filling to form triangles. With a fork, crimp the edges to seal them. Place the pastries on the prepared pan, spacing them evenly.

5. Cut two or three small slits into the top of each turnover. Brush with the egg and sprinkle the Parmesan on top.

6. Bake for 10 to 12 minutes, then remove from the oven. Check the pastries; if they are browning unevenly, rotate the pan. Return the pan to the oven and continue baking for another 10 minutes, or until the turnovers are golden brown.

7. Let cool for about 10 minutes before serving (the filling will be very hot).

HAM AND EGG CUPS

DAIRY-FREE OPTION | GLUTEN-FREE | ONE-PAN | UNDER 30 MINUTES

There's just something so cool about cooking eggs in ham "cups"—they're dead-easy yet impressive enough for the fanciest brunch. A convection oven crisps the edges of the ham while cooking the eggs quickly and perfectly. I like to serve these cups with toasted English muffins.

SERVES 6

Prep Time: 10 minutes

Cook Time: 15 minutes

Nonstick cooking spray

6 thin slices ham

6 large eggs

Kosher salt

Freshly ground black pepper

2 tablespoons finely grated Parmesan cheese (see the Simple Swap tip for a dairy-free option)

SIMPLE SWAP: For a dairy-free version, replace the cheese with a teaspoon of panko bread crumbs mixed with a little olive oil (it protects the egg yolk from overcooking).

1. Select Convection Roast and preheat the oven to 375°F.

2. Spray the cups of a 6-cup muffin tin with cooking spray. Press a slice of ham into each cup, smoothing out the sides as much as possible. The ham should extend over the top of the cup by ¼ to ½ inch. Crack an egg into each cup and season with salt and pepper. Top each yolk with 1 teaspoon of the cheese.

3. Bake for 5 minutes, then slide out the rack and check the eggs. They should just be starting to firm up and turn opaque. Rotate the muffin tin if the eggs are cooking unevenly.

4. Cook for another 5 minutes and check again; if the egg whites are cooked through, remove the tin from the oven. The total cook time is about 12 minutes for fully cooked whites and runny yolks; if you prefer the yolks more done, cook for an additional minute or two.

5. When the eggs are cooked as desired, remove the muffin tin and let cool for a couple of minutes. Run a thin knife around the ham and use a spoon to remove the cups.

SMOKED SALMON AND MIXED HERB FRITTATA

GLUTEN-FREE | UNDER 30 MINUTES

A frittata is the perfect way to make fancy eggs for a crowd. No flipping and folding as with a French omelet, and no need to worry about timing because frittatas are good either warm or at room temperature. Add a simple salad and some bread, and you've got brunch.

SERVES 4

Prep Time: 15 minutes

Cook Time: 15 minutes

2 tablespoons unsalted butter

¼ cup chopped onion

8 large eggs

½ teaspoon kosher salt

¼ cup whole milk

2 tablespoons chopped
fresh dill

2 tablespoons chopped
fresh chives

1 tablespoon chopped
fresh parsley

3 ounces smoked salmon,
flaked or chopped

½ cup grated
mozzarella cheese

¼ teaspoon freshly ground
black pepper

1. Select Convection Roast and preheat the oven to 375°F.

2. In an oven-safe nonstick or cast-iron skillet, heat the butter over medium-high heat until foaming. Add the onion and cook, stirring occasionally, for about 5 minutes, or until soft.

3. While the onion cooks, whisk the eggs with the salt in a medium bowl. Let sit for a minute or two, then add the milk and whisk again until the eggs are thoroughly mixed with no streaks of white remaining, but not foamy. Stir in the dill, chives, and parsley.

4. Distribute the salmon evenly over the bottom of the skillet with the onion. Pour the egg mixture into the pan. Let the eggs cook, undisturbed, for 5 to 7 minutes, until the edges are set. The center will still be quite liquid. If the frittata begins to form large bubbles on the bottom, use a silicone spatula to break them up.

5. Run a silicone spatula around the edges of the frittata. Transfer the skillet to the oven and bake for about 2 minutes, until the center is just set. Remove the skillet from the oven and sprinkle the cheese over the top. Return the pan to the oven and bake for another 1 to 2 minutes, until the cheese is melted and very slightly browned. Sprinkle the pepper over the frittata.

6. Let the frittata rest for 1 to 2 minutes. To serve, either divide the frittata into four wedges in the skillet, or run the spatula around the edges again and slide the whole frittata out onto a plate before cutting it into wedges. Serve warm or at room temperature.

SIMPLE SWAP: Frittatas are perfect for using up leftovers—pretty much any cooked vegetables or meats can replace the salmon and herbs.

HOME FRIES WITH BACON AND EGGS

DAIRY-FREE | GLUTEN-FREE | ONE-PAN

Who says you need to stand over a hot skillet for home fries? These fries cook on a sheet pan, so you can relax while the convection oven does the work. Add eggs, and you've got a hearty breakfast with very little work.

SERVES 4

Prep Time: 10 minutes

Cook Time: 25 minutes

2 medium Yukon gold potatoes, peeled and cut into ¼-inch cubes (about 3 cups)

1 medium onion, chopped (about 1 cup)

⅓ cup diced red or green bell pepper

1 tablespoon vegetable oil

½ teaspoon kosher salt, divided

¼ teaspoon freshly ground black pepper, divided

12 ounces thick-sliced bacon, cut into ¼-inch pieces

4 large eggs

SIMPLE SWAP: For a vegetarian version, leave out the bacon and add about 8 ounces of quartered mushrooms to the potato mixture.

1. Select Convection Roast and preheat the oven to 375°F.

2. Put the potatoes, onion, and bell pepper on a sheet pan. Drizzle with the oil, ¼ teaspoon of salt, and ⅛ teaspoon of pepper and toss to coat. Spread the vegetables out in a single layer as much as possible. Scatter the bacon pieces evenly over the top.

3. Bake for 10 minutes, then remove the pan from the oven and stir the potato mixture. Return to the oven and bake for another 10 minutes, or until the potatoes are tender inside and beginning to crisp on the outside, and the bacon is becoming crisp.

4. Remove the pan from the oven. Using a large spoon, create four circular openings in the potato mixture. Gently crack an egg into each opening; season the eggs with the remaining ¼ teaspoon of salt and ⅛ teaspoon of pepper. Return the pan to the oven and bake for 3 minutes for very runny yolks or up to 8 minutes for firm yolks.

5. Use a spatula to transfer the eggs from the pan to four separate plates, then scoop out the home fries to serve on the side.

FOR COUNTERTOP OVENS: The potato mixture will be more crowded on a smaller sheet pan, so you'll want to stir it several times to ensure even browning.

FRENCH TOAST CASSEROLE WITH SAUSAGE LINKS

Cooking batches of French toast while keeping an eye on a skillet of sausages requires speed and agility. Not so with this dish!

SERVES 4

Prep Time: 15 minutes

Cook Time: 30 minutes

6 fresh breakfast sausage links

4 large eggs

1½ cups whole milk

½ teaspoon kosher salt

5 tablespoons pure maple syrup, divided

5 or 6 thick slices of stale bread, cut into 1-inch cubes

SIMPLE SWAP: If you have bulk fresh breakfast sausage instead of links, just brown it on the stovetop, breaking it up into chunks. You can either stir it into the bread mixture or layer it on top so it gets browned and crisp.

1. Select Convection Roast and preheat the oven to 375°F.

2. Put the sausage links in a Dutch oven and bake for about 15 minutes, until lightly browned. They may not be cooked all the way through, but they will cook again. You just want to render some of their fat.

3. Meanwhile, in a medium bowl, whisk the eggs until completely mixed. Add the milk, salt, and 1 tablespoon of maple syrup and whisk to combine. Add the bread cubes and gently stir to coat with the egg mixture. Let sit for 2 to 3 minutes to let the bread absorb some of the custard, then gently stir again.

4. After the sausages have browned, remove the Dutch oven. Turn the oven to Convection Bake and reduce the temperature to 350°F. Transfer the sausages to a plate. If there is more than a thin coat of fat on the bottom of the pot, pour out the excess.

5. Pour the bread mixture into the Dutch oven, then top with the sausage links.

6. Bake for 30 minutes, or until the sausages are browned and a knife inserted into the center of the casserole comes out clean.

7. Serve with the remaining 4 tablespoons of maple syrup.

MEXICAN-STYLE CORN ON THE COB page 32

VEGETABLES, SIDES, AND APPETIZERS

ROASTED TRI-COLOR PEPPER SALAD

GLUTEN-FREE | VEGETARIAN

Most recipes for roasting peppers call for cooking the peppers whole and turning them several times to get all the sides charred. But if you cut them into pieces before broiling, they cook faster and are much less messy. This salad is a great way to showcase roasted peppers. A simple dressing with salty capers and cheese perfectly complements their sweet complexity.

SERVES 4

Prep Time: 15 minutes,
  plus 1 hour to chill

Cook Time: 5 minutes

4 bell peppers, a combination of red, yellow, and orange

3 tablespoons chopped fresh flat-leaf parsley

2 small garlic cloves, minced

4 teaspoons sherry vinegar

½ teaspoon Dijon mustard

¼ cup extra-virgin olive oil

3 cups bitter greens, such as arugula, watercress, or a spring mix

3 tablespoons drained capers

2 tablespoons crumbled ricotta salata or feta cheese

1. Place the top oven rack in the highest position. Select Convection Broil and set to High if possible.

2. Remove the stems from the peppers and cut each into 2 or 3 flat pieces. Remove the seeds and ribs.

3. Place the peppers on a sheet pan, skin-side up. Broil for 4 to 5 minutes, until the skins are almost completely charred. (If your broiler does not have a high setting, this may take a few minutes longer.) Transfer the pieces to a glass or metal bowl and pour any pan juices over them. Cover the bowl with a plate (or plastic wrap or aluminum foil). Let the peppers steam and cool for 10 minutes.

4. Remove the peppers from the bowl. Drain any accumulated liquid into a separate small bowl. Peel the burned skins off the peppers. Cut the peppers into ½-inch strips and return them to their original bowl. Add the parsley.

5. Add the garlic, vinegar, and mustard to the reserved liquid from the peppers and whisk until smooth. Drizzle in the oil while continuing to whisk. Pour the dressing over the peppers. Cover and refrigerate for at least 1 hour and up to 2 days.

6. Divide the greens among 6 plates. Drape the pepper strips over the greens, drizzle with a little vinaigrette, and sprinkle with the capers. Top with the cheese and serve.

SAVE FOR LATER: If you have more marinated peppers than you need for the salad, save them for easy appetizers (they'll last several days in the refrigerator). Just bring them to room temperature, chop coarsely, and use to top crostini or bruschetta.

ROASTED MUSHROOMS

DAIRY-FREE | GLUTEN-FREE | VEGAN | ONE-PAN

Some recipe writers still claim that you should never wash mushrooms because they will soak up all the water and become soggy. But mushrooms are mostly water to begin with, so wash off the dirt before you roast them. Their liquid will evaporate, and you'll have beautifully browned mushrooms.

SERVES 4

Prep Time: 10 minutes

Cook Time: 35 minutes

1 pound cremini or button mushrooms, trimmed and quartered (or cut into eighths if very large)

2 to 3 tablespoons vegetable oil

½ teaspoon kosher salt

1 or 2 garlic cloves, minced (optional)

SAVE FOR LATER: These mushrooms are a great ingredient to have on hand for quick meals throughout the week. Add them to a Smoked Salmon and Mixed Herb Frittata (page 22) or use as a topping for Thin-Crust Pizza (page 126).

1. Select Convection Roast and preheat the oven to 400°F.

2. Put the mushrooms on a sheet pan and drizzle with the oil. Toss to coat and sprinkle with the salt.

3. Roast the mushrooms for about 15 minutes, then remove them from the oven. Move the mushrooms from the outer edges to the center of the pan and vice versa. Return to the oven and roast for about 15 minutes more. The mushrooms should be lightly browned and shrunken in size. If you prefer them more browned and concentrated in flavor, roast for another 10 to 15 minutes.

4. Add the garlic (if using) and toss to distribute evenly. Return the pan to the oven for 3 to 5 minutes, until the garlic is softened and fragrant.

FOR COUNTERTOP OVENS: If you put a whole pound of mushrooms on a small sheet pan, they'll be crowded, and the liquid they release may not be able to evaporate fully. That's okay. When you check them at 15 minutes, if you see a pool of liquid, just drain or blot it off before continuing. That way, the mushrooms will be able to brown nicely.

SWEET AND SOUR ROASTED BRUSSELS SPROUTS

DAIRY-FREE | GLUTEN-FREE | VEGAN

If you're old enough, you probably remember Brussels sprouts as very bitter and—frankly—stinky. That's not your imagination; they really did taste and smell of sulfur. But in the 1990s, scientists and botanists in the Netherlands worked on breeding sprouts with fewer of those nasty compounds, and they succeeded. If you haven't tried Brussels sprouts since you were a kid, you might want to give this recipe a try.

SERVES 4

Prep Time: 10 minutes

Cook Time: 30 minutes

2 pounds Brussels sprouts

2 to 3 tablespoons
    vegetable oil

1 teaspoon kosher salt

¼ cup balsamic vinegar

2 tablespoons brown sugar

Freshly ground black pepper

SIMPLE SWAP: Not a fan of Brussels sprouts? Try this with broccoli florets instead. They usually take slightly less time than sprouts, so check them at 15 minutes.

1. Select Convection Roast and preheat the oven to 375°F.

2. Trim the ends of the Brussels sprouts and peel off any damaged outer leaves. Cut the sprouts in half through the stem end.

3. Put the sprouts on a sheet pan and drizzle with the oil, stirring to coat evenly. Sprinkle with the salt. Arrange the sprouts cut-side down.

4. Roast for 20 minutes, or just until crisp-tender.

5. Meanwhile, stir together the balsamic vinegar, brown sugar, and pepper until the sugar dissolves.

6. Remove the sprouts from the oven and pour the balsamic mixture over them. Toss to coat and return to the oven for another 10 minutes, until tender, browned, and glazed.

FOR COUNTERTOP OVENS: You may not be able to fit all the sprouts cut-side down on a smaller sheet pan, but just do your best. If you like, stir halfway through and arrange the rest cut-side down for the remaining time.

MEXICAN-STYLE CORN ON THE COB

GLUTEN-FREE | VEGETARIAN | **ONE-PAN** | UNDER 30 MINUTES

Known as elotes, Mexican "street corn" is sold by vendors throughout Mexico and even in some US cities. It's roasted or grilled, coated with mayonnaise and a dry, aged cheese called cotija, then finished with a squeeze of lime and a sprinkling of chili powder.

SERVES 4

Prep Time: 10 minutes

Cook Time: 20 minutes

4 ears corn, shucked

1 tablespoon vegetable oil

¼ cup mayonnaise

½ cup crumbled cotija cheese or grated Parmesan cheese

2 teaspoons Mexican chili powder (see Simple Swap tip), plus more to serve

1 lime, quartered

1. Select Convection Roast and preheat the oven to 350°F.

2. Put the corn on a sheet pan and coat with the oil. Roast for 15 to 20 minutes, or until the kernels are tender and beginning to brown. Let the corn cool for about 5 minutes.

3. Insert corn holders into the ears of corn (or if you have short skewers or ice pop sticks, you can insert those in one end of the corn). Spread each ear of corn with a thin layer of mayonnaise to coat, then sprinkle the cheese and chili powder all over each ear. Serve with lime wedges and additional chili powder.

SAVE FOR LATER: If you like, roast eight ears of corn and save the rest for another meal. You can cut the kernels off the cobs and toss them with the same ingredients for a Mexican street corn salad called esquites, or stir them into salsa.

SIMPLE SWAP: Tajin and Valentina are brand names of a common Mexican spice mix with salt, ground chiles, and dried lime, but if you can't find them, you can use ground ancho chile or even regular chili powder.

ROASTED CARROTS WITH CUMIN-ORANGE VINAIGRETTE

DAIRY-FREE | GLUTEN-FREE | VEGAN

Roasting carrots concentrates their flavor, bringing out a sweet earthiness. If you can find true baby carrots—that is, small thin carrots usually sold with their greens intact, not the bags of carrots peeled and whittled down to bite-size pieces—they make a great presentation. But regular carrots, cut into equal lengths, are just as delicious.

SERVES 4

Prep Time: 10 minutes

Cook Time: 30 minutes

2 pounds carrots

2 tablespoons vegetable oil

2 teaspoons kosher salt, divided

½ teaspoon cumin seeds

2 tablespoons extra-virgin olive oil

2 tablespoons orange juice

2 tablespoons chopped fresh mint

SIMPLE SWAP: If you don't have whole cumin seeds, just whisk ½ teaspoon of ground cumin into the vinaigrette.

1. Select Convection Roast and preheat the oven to 400°F.

2. Peel the carrots and cut into 3-inch pieces. The pieces should be about ½-inch thick (about the size of a finger), so halve them lengthwise if medium-size or quarter them if large. Put the carrots on a sheet pan and drizzle with the vegetable oil and 1 teaspoon of salt. Toss to coat.

3. Roast for 15 minutes, then toss and roast for another 15 to 20 minutes, or until tender and browned in spots.

4. Meanwhile, crush the cumin seeds with a heavy skillet or a mortar and pestle, or pulse briefly in a spice grinder until broken up but not powdery. When the carrots are done, turn off the oven. Sprinkle the cumin seeds over the carrots and return them to the oven for 30 to 60 seconds, just until the cumin is fragrant.

5. In a small bowl, whisk together the olive oil, orange juice, and remaining 1 teaspoon of salt. Drizzle the vinaigrette over the carrots and sprinkle with the mint. Serve warm or at room temperature.

CAULIFLOWER DAUPHINOISE

GLUTEN-FREE | VEGETARIAN | ONE-PAN

Potatoes Dauphinoise is an ultra-rich, creamy gratin topped with cheese. I've substituted sliced cauliflower for the potatoes to please both lovers of that vegetable and those who must limit their carbohydrate intake. Made all in one pan, this recipe is easy, elegant, and delicious.

SERVES 6 TO 8

Prep Time: 15 minutes

Cook Time: 30 minutes

---

1 cup heavy (whipping) cream

½ cup whole milk

3 garlic cloves, lightly smashed

1 thyme sprig

1 parsley sprig

1 small head cauliflower

1½ teaspoons kosher salt

¼ teaspoon freshly ground black pepper

4 ounces Gruyère cheese, grated

SIMPLE SWAP: You can, of course, use sliced potatoes, or a combination of potatoes and cauliflower. The cooking time remains the same.

1. Select Convection Roast and preheat the oven to 350°F.

2. Pour the cream and milk into a large cast-iron skillet or other oven-safe skillet. Add the garlic, thyme, and parsley and bring to a simmer. Keep at a low simmer while you prepare the cauliflower.

3. Using a mandoline, V-slicer, or knife, slice the cauliflower ¼-inch thick, cutting any large slices into bite-size pieces. Don't worry if some of the cauliflower breaks into small bits.

4. Remove the herb sprigs and garlic cloves from the cream mixture. Add the cauliflower, salt, and pepper and stir very gently just to cover the cauliflower with the cream. Spread into an even layer. Sprinkle the cheese evenly over the top.

5. Transfer the pan to the center rack of the oven and bake until the cauliflower is tender, 30 to 35 minutes.

6. Switch the oven to Convection Broil. Leave the pan on the center rack and broil just until the cheese is lightly browned.

GREEN BEANS WITH SHALLOTS AND PANCETTA

DAIRY-FREE | GLUTEN-FREE | **ONE-PAN** | UNDER 30 MINUTES

A modern version of green beans simmered with onions and bacon, these roasted beans make a quick and easy but hearty side dish. The beans collapse a little and concentrate in flavor, while the shallots become soft and sweet as they roast.

SERVES 4

Prep Time: 15 minutes

Cook Time: 15 minutes

1½ pounds green beans

2 large shallots, cut into rings

2 tablespoons vegetable oil

½ teaspoon kosher salt

2 ounces pancetta, diced

1. Select Convection Roast and preheat the oven to 400°F.

2. Put the beans and shallots on a sheet pan. Drizzle with the oil and toss to coat. Spread into a single layer as much as possible. Season with the salt. Scatter the pancetta over the beans.

3. Roast for about 7 minutes, then stir the mixture. Continue roasting until the beans are browned and tender and the pancetta is crisp, another 7 to 8 minutes.

HELPFUL HACK: For quicker, easier cleanup, line the sheet pan with a silicone baking mat before roasting.

SIMPLE SWAP: If you can't find pancetta, substitute diced thick-cut bacon.

CRISPY PARMESAN POTATOES

GLUTEN-FREE | VEGETARIAN

For these extra crisp potatoes, use small spuds—no more than about 1½ inches in diameter. You can find tiny potatoes in multiple colors in any grocery store.

SERVES 4

Prep Time: 15 minutes,
   plus 10 minutes to cool
Cook Time: 35 minutes

2 tablespoons kosher salt

1½ pounds small red or gold
   potatoes (1 to 1½ inches
   in diameter)

3 to 5 tablespoons
   vegetable oil

¼ cup grated Parmesan
   cheese, or more

½ teaspoon freshly ground
   black pepper

EVEN EASIER: If you don't have time for boiling and smashing the potatoes, you can still make deliciously crisp potatoes. Cut them in half and toss with the oil. Sprinkle with 1 teaspoon of salt. Arrange them cut-side down on a sheet pan and roast for 30 to 35 minutes. Sprinkle with the Parmesan and pepper.

1. Select Convection Roast and preheat the oven to 400°F.

2. Bring a large saucepan of water to a boil over medium-high heat. Add the salt and potatoes and boil for 12 to 15 minutes, until tender. Drain the potatoes and allow to cool for 10 minutes.

3. Generously coat a sheet pan with oil. Place the potatoes on the pan, spacing them evenly. Use a paring knife to cut a ¼-inch-deep "X" in the top of each potato. (This helps keep them from breaking apart when smashing.)

4. Coat the bottom of a heavy drinking glass or sturdy spatula with oil. Use the glass or spatula to gently smash the potatoes to about a ½-inch thickness, ensuring that the potatoes don't break into pieces.

5. Brush the tops of the potatoes lightly with oil.

6. Roast for 15 to 20 minutes, until the potatoes are crisp and golden brown. For extra crisp potatoes, carefully flip them halfway through cooking. Remove the pan from the oven and sprinkle the potatoes with the Parmesan and pepper. Serve immediately.

FOR COUNTERTOP OVENS: It may be difficult to fit 1½ pounds of potatoes on a small sheet pan; you may want to cut the amount to 1 pound. As you smash them, slide them to the side so you have room to smash the rest, then arrange them evenly on the pan.

PROSCIUTTO-WRAPPED ASPARAGUS WITH BALSAMIC VINEGAR

DAIRY-FREE | GLUTEN-FREE | **ONE-PAN** | UNDER 30 MINUTES

Asparagus spears wrapped in prosciutto makes for an easy, elegant first course or appetizer. Tangy aged balsamic vinegar is the perfect complement to the salty ham.

SERVES 4

Prep Time: 15 minutes

Cook Time: 10 minutes

6 to 8 thin slices Prosciutto di Parma or serrano ham (about 4 ounces)

1 pound asparagus, trimmed

2 teaspoons aged balsamic vinegar (see Simple Swap tip)

1. Select Convection Roast and preheat the oven to 375°F.

2. Cut the prosciutto into long strips (one strip per asparagus spear). Starting at the bottom of the spear, wrap each piece of asparagus about halfway to two-thirds of the way up with a strip of prosciutto, wrapping at an angle. Place the wrapped spears on a sheet pan.

3. Roast the asparagus for 10 to 12 minutes, until the asparagus is tender and the prosciutto is crisp. Very thick spears may take longer.

4. Transfer the asparagus to a platter. Drizzle with the balsamic vinegar. Serve warm or at room temperature.

SIMPLE SWAP: Use a vinegar that's thick enough to coat the inside of the bottle as you tip it up; I find Villa Manodori vinegar to be reasonably priced for the quality. If you don't have a thick, aged balsamic and don't want to invest in a bottle, you can use a regular non-aged version. Pour about ¼ cup into a small saucepan and bring to a boil. Simmer until thickened to a syrup consistency.

HELPFUL HACK: If you buy a package of prosciutto already sliced, the slices are usually separated by sheets of plastic or wax paper. If so, leave them intact and cut into strips with scissors. Then you can peel the strips off the plastic as you need them.

SPICY MEXICAN-STYLE CROSTINI

VEGETARIAN | UNDER 30 MINUTES

If you like nachos but hate soggy chips and tough, leathery cheese, molletes are the snack for you. Spicy beans and cheese top crisp bread slices, which quickly turn hot and melty in the convection oven. Pico de gallo is the finishing touch.

SERVES 4

Prep Time: 10 minutes

Cook Time: 10 minutes

---

1 small baguette, cut on the bias into ¾-inch slices (12 to 16 slices)

2 tablespoons vegetable oil, or more as needed

½ teaspoon kosher salt

1 (14-ounce) can black or pinto beans, drained but liquid reserved

1 tablespoon chili powder

6 ounces shredded Monterey Jack cheese, plain or with jalapeños

½ cup pico de gallo or other fresh salsa

1. Select Convection Roast and preheat the oven to 400°F.

2. Place the bread slices on a sheet pan. Use a basting brush to very lightly coat the bread slices with oil, then flip and brush the other sides. Sprinkle with the salt.

3. Roast until lightly browned and crisp, about 5 minutes.

4. Meanwhile, mash the beans with about half their liquid in a medium bowl. Stir in the chili powder. For completely smooth beans, use an immersion blender or food processor. For chunkier beans, use a potato masher.

5. When the bread is toasted, spread the beans over the slices, about ¼-inch thick. You may not need all the beans. Divide the cheese over the bean spread.

6. Return to the oven and roast for 5 to 7 minutes, until the cheese is bubbling and melted.

7. Let cool for a minute or two, then top with salsa and serve.

EVEN EASIER: Use canned refritos (refried beans) instead of mashing your own. You can also use unseasoned store-bought crostini instead of the baguette.

SMOKED SALMON PHYLLO TRIANGLES

UNDER 30 MINUTES

For an elegant appetizer, try these phyllo triangles filled with smoked salmon and cream cheese. Once you get the folding down, they come together easily, and they can be made well in advance and frozen for an (almost) instant savory snack.

SERVES 6

Prep Time: 15 minutes

Cook Time: 10 minutes

4 ounces smoked salmon, flaked or chopped

4 ounces cream cheese, softened

2 scallions, chopped

12 sheets phyllo dough, thawed

½ cup (1 stick) unsalted butter, melted

SAVE FOR LATER: The triangles can be assembled ahead of time and frozen in a zip-top bag. Bake the frozen triangles for 16 to 18 minutes.

SIMPLE SWAP: You can use just about anything to fill phyllo triangles; try the filling for the Ham and Cheese Pastries (page 20) or brie with chopped Roasted Mushrooms (page 30).

1. Select Convection Roast and preheat the oven to 400°F. Line a sheet pan with a silicone baking mat.

2. In a small bowl, mash the salmon, cream cheese, and scallions into a rough paste.

3. When you're ready to assemble the triangles, have the melted butter ready, and open the package of dough. Phyllo dries out easily, so don't open it until you're ready to use it. While assembling the triangles, cover the rest of the dough with plastic wrap to keep it from drying out.

4. Unfold the phyllo and cut each sheet lengthwise into two long strips (it's easiest to do this in two or three batches). Lay out 3 or 4 strips of phyllo on a cutting board with the short end toward you, and brush the strips lightly with melted butter. Using a small spoon, place about 2 teaspoons of the filling in the lower left corner of the phyllo. Spread it out so that it's roughly triangular and covers the corner. Wrap the phyllo up like a flag, using repeated diagonal folds. Place the finished triangle on the prepared sheet pan and brush with a little more butter.

5. Repeat with the remaining phyllo to make 24 triangles.

6. Bake for 10 to 12 minutes, until the dough is golden brown and flaky. Let cool for 5 to 7 minutes before serving.

MACARONI AND CHEESE WITH ROASTED RED PEPPERS AND AGED GOUDA

VEGETARIAN | UNDER 30 MINUTES

I grew up with macaroni and cheese served as a main dish. It wasn't until I moved to the South that I discovered it also makes a great side dish for roasted or grilled sausages, chops, or chicken. My version starts on the stovetop and finishes in a convection oven for a golden brown, crispy top.

SERVES 6 TO 8

Prep Time: 15 minutes

Cook Time: 15 minutes

FOR THE MACARONI

Kosher salt

1 (12-ounce) box elbow
macaroni or small shells

2 tablespoons unsalted butter,
plus more for greasing

2 tablespoons all-purpose flour

¼ teaspoon ground mustard

1½ cups whole milk

2 ounces cream cheese

9 ounces aged Gouda
cheese, shredded

3 ounces fontina or Monterey
Jack cheese, shredded

½ cup coarsely chopped
roasted red peppers

FOR THE TOPPING

2 tablespoons unsalted
butter, melted

1 cup panko bread crumbs

½ ounce aged Gouda cheese,
finely grated

1. **To make the macaroni:** Select Convection Roast and preheat the oven to 350°F. Lightly butter a 9-by-13-inch baking dish.

2. Bring a medium pot of salted water to a boil. Add the macaroni and cook according to the package directions. (If you like your pasta firm, remove it just before it's completely done because it will continue to cook in the sauce.) Drain and set aside.

3. Meanwhile, melt the butter in a medium saucepan over medium heat. Add the flour and mustard and stir to combine. Cook for 2 to 3 minutes, until the mixture is beige and thick but fairly smooth. Add half the milk and whisk until the mixture is smooth. Add the rest of the milk and whisk again. Let the sauce cook for a minute to thicken.

4. Reduce the heat to low. Add the cream cheese and stir just until melted. Add the Gouda and fontina in several batches, stirring until each batch is melted before adding the next. Taste and add salt if necessary. Remove the sauce from the heat.

5. Stir the drained pasta and the roasted red peppers into the sauce.

6. Pour the mixture into the prepared baking dish.

7. **To make the topping:** Mix together the butter and bread crumbs and stir to coat. Let cool slightly, then add the cheese. Stir to combine and sprinkle over the macaroni mixture. Bake for 13 to 15 minutes, until the cheese sauce is bubbling and the topping is golden brown and crisp.

SIMPLE SWAP: If you can't find aged Gouda, you can use aged Cheddar in the cheese sauce and Parmesan in the topping.

OVEN POLENTA WITH ROASTED TOMATOES

DAIRY-FREE OPTION | GLUTEN-FREE | VEGETARIAN | VEGAN OPTION

Starting polenta or grits on the stovetop and finishing in the oven is an easy, almost completely hands-off method for this hearty side dish, which is perfect with Italian-Style Meatloaf (page 88), meatballs, or Italian sausages. Roasted tomatoes and garlic make a delicious topping for the creamy grits.

SERVES 6 TO 8

Prep Time: 10 minutes

Cook Time: 40 minutes

2 cups vegetable broth

2 cups whole milk or additional vegetable broth

2 tablespoons unsalted butter or extra-virgin olive oil

1½ teaspoons kosher salt, divided

1 cup polenta or grits

2 pints cherry tomatoes, halved

4 large garlic cloves, sliced

¼ cup extra-virgin olive oil

2 ounces Parmesan cheese, finely grated (optional)

½ cup whole-milk ricotta (optional)

1. Select Convection Roast and preheat the oven to 325°F.

2. Bring the broth and milk to a simmer in a large, oven-safe saucepan over medium-high heat. Add the butter and ¾ teaspoon of salt and whisk to dissolve the salt. Add the polenta, whisking as you pour it in. Return the mixture to a low boil, immediately cover, and transfer to the oven.

3. Bake for 15 minutes, then stir. Cover and return to the oven until the polenta is tender, another 15 to 20 minutes.

4. Meanwhile, in a large bowl, toss the tomatoes and garlic with the oil. Transfer to a sheet pan and arrange in a single layer. Sprinkle with the remaining ¾ teaspoon of salt.

5. Remove the polenta from the oven. Increase the oven temperature to 425°F.

6. When the oven is up to temperature, put the sheet pan in the oven and roast for 10 to 12 minutes, until the tomatoes are collapsing and the garlic is golden brown.

7. Meanwhile, whisk the polenta vigorously, scraping the bottom of the pan, until it's smooth and thick. Gradually add the Parmesan and ricotta (if using), stirring until incorporated. Cover and keep warm over low heat while the tomatoes finish roasting.

8. Remove the tomatoes from the oven. Serve the polenta in bowls, topped with the tomatoes.

SIMPLE SWAP: Instead of tomatoes, top this polenta with chopped Roasted Mushrooms (page 30).

CURRY CHICKEN WINGS

GLUTEN-FREE

Think you can't get crisp chicken wings without frying? You can. Tossing wings with salt and baking powder, especially if you can let them sit and dry out slightly, will produce amazingly brown and crisp results.

SERVES 8

Prep Time: 10 minutes

Cook Time: 30 minutes

2 pounds chicken wing flats and drumettes (16 to 20 pieces)

1½ teaspoons kosher salt

1½ teaspoons baking powder

4 tablespoons (½ stick) unsalted butter

2 teaspoons Worcestershire sauce

2 teaspoons curry powder

½ teaspoon granulated garlic

¼ teaspoon paprika

2 dashes hot sauce

SIMPLE SWAP: Once the wings are roasted, you can use your favorite sauce instead of the curry. Hot sauce and butter is traditional, but Thai sweet chili sauce is another great option.

1. Select Convection Roast and preheat the oven to 425°F. Line a sheet pan with aluminum foil and set a rack on top.

2. Put the wings in a large bowl.

3. In a small bowl, stir together the salt and baking powder. Sprinkle the mixture over the wings and, using your hands, toss thoroughly to coat. If you have time, let the wings sit for 20 minutes or up to 1 hour.

4. While the wings sit, prepare the sauce. Melt the butter in a small saucepan. Add the Worcestershire sauce, curry powder, garlic, paprika, and hot sauce and stir to combine. Keep warm.

5. Place the wings on the prepared rack, making sure they're not touching. Roast for 15 minutes. Wash the large bowl and set aside.

6. Remove the pan from the oven. Using tongs, turn the wings over. Rotate the pan and return to the oven to continue roasting for 12 to 15 minutes. The wings should be dark golden brown and a bit charred in places.

7. Transfer the wings to the bowl. Pour the warm sauce over the wings and toss to coat. Serve immediately, with lots of napkins.

SALMON AND VEGETABLE PARCHMENT PACKETS page 54

SEAFOOD

SHRIMP FAJITAS

DAIRY-FREE | GLUTEN-FREE OPTION | **ONE-PAN** | UNDER 30 MINUTES

Making fajitas in the oven is about as easy as dinner can get. The only tricky part is making sure you don't overcook the shrimp, but if you use the right size, and give the peppers and onions a head start, the shrimp will cook perfectly in the time it takes to set the table.

SERVES 4

Prep Time: 10 minutes

Cook Time: 10 minutes

8 (6-inch) flour or corn tortillas

1 red bell pepper, cut into
½-inch-thick slices

1 green bell pepper, cut into
½-inch-thick slices

1 jalapeño pepper, seeded and
cut into ⅛-inch-thick slices

1 medium onion, cut into
½-inch-thick wedges

3 tablespoons vegetable
oil, divided

2 tablespoons Mexican or fajita
seasoning, divided

1 teaspoon kosher salt, divided

1½ pounds large shrimp
(21 to 26 per pound), peeled
and deveined

1 small avocado, sliced,
for serving

Salsa, for serving

1. Select Convection Roast and preheat the oven to 375°F.

2. Wrap the tortillas tightly in a large sheet of aluminum foil.

3. Put the bell peppers, jalapeño, and onion on a large sheet pan and drizzle with 2 tablespoons of oil. Sprinkle with 1 tablespoon of Mexican seasoning and ½ teaspoon of salt and toss to coat.

4. Place the sheet pan on the upper rack and the tortillas on the lower rack.

5. Roast for 5 minutes, then remove the sheet pan from the oven. Stir the vegetables and move them to the outer edges of the pan. Place the shrimp in the center of the pan and drizzle with the remaining 1 tablespoon of oil. Sprinkle with the remaining 1 tablespoon of Mexican seasoning and ½ teaspoon of salt. Stir to distribute the seasonings evenly.

6. Continue roasting for 5 to 6 minutes, until the vegetables are soft and browned in places and the shrimp are opaque. Remove the sheet pan and tortillas from the oven.

7. Spoon the fajita mixture into the tortillas. Serve with avocado slices and salsa.

FOR COUNTERTOP OVENS: Unless your oven has space for two racks, you'll need to heat the tortillas separately. Place the foil packet in the oven as it preheats and for about 5 minutes after the oven is heated. Then move the foil packet to the top of the oven to keep the tortillas warm while you roast the fajita mixture.

SHRIMP SCAMPI WITH WILTED ARUGULA

GLUTEN-FREE | **ONE-PAN** | UNDER 30 MINUTES

Serve this garlicky shrimp scampi with crusty bread to sop up the sauce.

SERVES 4

Prep Time: 10 minutes

Cook Time: 5 minutes

4 tablespoons (½ stick) unsalted butter

2 tablespoons extra-virgin olive oil

1 teaspoon kosher salt

6 garlic cloves, minced

¼ cup chopped fresh parsley, divided

2 pounds large shrimp (21 to 26 per pound), peeled and deveined

2 tablespoons freshly squeezed lemon juice

1 (9- to 10-ounce) bag arugula

1. Select Convection Roast and preheat the oven to 375°F. Put the butter in a 9-by-13-inch baking pan, and place the pan in the oven while the oven heats.

2. When the butter has melted, remove the pan from the oven and add the oil, salt, garlic, and half the parsley. Stir well. Add the shrimp and toss to coat, then arrange the shrimp in a single layer. Roast for 5 minutes. Check the shrimp; they should be opaque and pink. If they are not quite done, cook for another minute.

3. Remove the pan from the oven. Add the lemon juice, arugula, and remaining parsley. Toss well to wilt the arugula. Serve immediately.

SIMPLE SWAP: You can use baby spinach instead of arugula.

BACON-WRAPPED HERB-STUFFED TROUT

DAIRY-FREE | GLUTEN-FREE

Trout can easily overcook in a hot oven, but wrapping it in bacon provides protection as well as great flavor and texture. Roasted potatoes and steamed or roasted green beans make excellent accompaniments.

SERVES 4

Prep Time: 15 minutes

Cook Time: 20 minutes

4 (8- to 10-ounce) rainbow trout, butterflied and boned

2 teaspoons kosher salt, divided

1 tablespoon extra-virgin olive oil, divided

1 tablespoon freshly squeezed lemon juice, divided

2 tablespoons chopped fresh parsley, divided

2 tablespoons chopped fresh chives, divided

8 thin bacon slices

Lemon wedges, for serving

1. Select Convection Roast and preheat the oven to 400°F. Lightly oil a sheet pan and place it in the oven as it preheats.

2. Sprinkle the inside and outside of each trout with the salt. Brush the inside with the oil and drizzle with the lemon juice. Scatter the parsley and chives on one side of each butterflied trout. Fold the trout closed and wrap each one with two slices of bacon.

3. Remove the pan from the oven and place the trout on it. Roast for 20 to 25 minutes, flipping halfway through, until the bacon is crisp. Serve with lemon wedges.

SIMPLE SWAP: If you can't find butterflied trout, stack two trout fillets flesh-side together and wrap in the bacon.

CRAB ENCHILADAS

GLUTEN-FREE

Enchiladas Suizas, made with a creamy, green chile–based sauce, originated in Mexico City in the 1950s. The name (meaning "Swiss-style enchiladas") supposedly derives from the liberal use of cream and cheese, which is not typical in most enchiladas. Using a good-quality tomatillo salsa for the sauce cuts down on prep time (I like Frontera brand).

SERVES 4

Prep Time: 15 minutes

Cook Time: 25 minutes

---

8 (6-inch) corn tortillas

Nonstick cooking spray or vegetable oil, for brushing

2 cups mild tomatillo salsa or green enchilada sauce

½ cup heavy (whipping) cream

8 ounces lump crabmeat, picked through to remove any shells

3 or 4 scallions, chopped

8 ounces Monterey Jack cheese, shredded

1. Select Convection Roast and preheat the oven to 350°F.

2. Spray the tortillas on both sides with cooking spray or brush lightly with oil. Arrange on a sheet pan, overlapping as little as possible. Bake for 5 minutes, or until warm and flexible.

3. Meanwhile, stir together the salsa and cream in a shallow, microwave-safe bowl and heat in the microwave until very warm, about 45 seconds.

4. Pour a quarter of the salsa mixture into a 9-by-13-inch baking dish. Place a tortilla in the sauce, turning it over to coat thoroughly. Spoon a heaping tablespoon of crab down the middle of the tortilla, then top with a teaspoon of scallions and a heaping tablespoon of cheese. Roll up the tortilla and place it seam-side down at one end of the pan. Repeat with the remaining tortillas, forming a row of enchiladas in the pan. Spoon most or all of the remaining sauce over the enchiladas so they are nicely coated but not drowning. Sprinkle the remaining cheese over the top.

5. Bake for 18 to 20 minutes, until the cheese is melted and the sauce is bubbling.

FOR COUNTERTOP OVENS: Warm the tortillas in two batches, filling and rolling the first batch while the second one heats.

SIMPLE SWAP: Use chopped cooked shrimp or chicken instead of crab.

SALMON AND VEGETABLE PARCHMENT PACKETS

GLUTEN-FREE | ONE-PAN | UNDER 30 MINUTES

Cooking individual servings of fish and vegetables in parchment paper is fast and makes cleanup a breeze. If you have kids, let them create their own packets—it's a great way to get them involved in dinner prep.

SERVES 4

Prep Time: 15 minutes

Cook Time: 10 minutes

---

4 teaspoons (½ stick) unsalted butter, at room temperature, divided

4 (6- to 8-ounce) skinless salmon fillets

1 teaspoon kosher salt, divided

Freshly ground black pepper

1 tablespoon very finely minced shallot or scallion, divided

1 small tomato, seeded and diced (about ½ cup), divided

1 cup chopped or sliced Roasted Mushrooms (page 30)

¾ cup frozen peas, thawed

2 tablespoons chopped fresh parsley

1. Select Convection Roast and preheat the oven to 425°F.

2. Cut four pieces of parchment paper the size of your sheet pan.

3. For each packet, smear 1 teaspoon of butter in the center of the parchment paper, spreading it out enough for the salmon to fit on the buttered portion. Season each side of the salmon generously with salt and several grinds of pepper, and place it on the butter.

4. Sprinkle the shallot and tomato over each salmon fillet. Scatter the mushrooms and peas around the salmon, and sprinkle the parsley over everything.

5. Lift the longer sides of the parchment so the edges meet right above the salmon, like a tent. Fold the edges over several times, leaving some air space over the fish and vegetables. You'll have what looks like a long tube filled with fish and vegetables. Fold the open ends over toward the fish a few times, crimping the folds tightly with your fingers. If necessary, use metal paper clips to secure the folded ends.

6. Set the packets on a sheet pan and bake for 8 to 11 minutes, depending on the thickness of the fish: 8 minutes for a piece less than 1-inch thick, 10 minutes for 1 inch, and 11 minutes for a thicker piece.

7. To serve, carefully transfer the packets to dinner plates and unfold or cut the parchment open. Alternatively, unfold or cut the parchment while the packets are still on the sheet pan, and slide the fish and vegetables onto each plate.

FOR COUNTERTOP OVENS: Some oven manuals say not to use parchment paper at high temperatures because it can get too close to the top heating element. If your manual gives this warning, use aluminum foil instead.

SIMPLE SWAP: You can use any cooked vegetables you like in the packets, but avoid raw vegetables, as they won't cook through all the way.

SLOW-ROASTED SALMON, SPINACH, AND BEANS

DAIRY-FREE | GLUTEN-FREE | ONE-PAN

Cooking salmon at a relatively low temperature results in a silky texture. The flavorful bed of beans and greens makes this salmon an easy, one-pan weeknight dinner.

SERVES 4

Prep Time: 10 minutes

Cook Time: 30 minutes

2 tablespoons olive oil, divided

1 garlic clove, thinly sliced

1 (9- to 10-ounce) bag baby spinach

1 (15-ounce) can cannellini or navy beans, rinsed and drained

1½ teaspoons kosher salt, divided

½ teaspoon ground cumin

½ teaspoon ground coriander

¼ teaspoon red pepper flakes

4 (6-ounce) skinless salmon fillets

1. Select Convection Roast and preheat the oven to 300°F.

2. Heat 1 tablespoon of oil in a large, oven-safe skillet over medium-high heat. Add the garlic and cook, stirring, until fragrant, about 30 seconds. Add the spinach a handful at a time and cook, tossing, until slightly wilted, adding more as you have room. Stir in the beans, ¾ teaspoon of salt, cumin, coriander, and red pepper flakes.

3. Season the salmon with the remaining ¾ teaspoon of salt. Place the fillets in a single layer on top of the spinach mixture and drizzle with the remaining 1 tablespoon of oil.

4. Roast until the salmon is opaque in the center, 30 to 35 minutes.

FOR COUNTERTOP OVENS: Make sure your skillet will fit in the oven; if not, transfer the beans and spinach to a baking dish after sautéing.

TILAPIA AND RICE WITH MUSHROOM SAUCE

ONE-PAN | UNDER 30 MINUTES

This creamy but light sauce turns everyday fish and rice into a decadent company-worthy entrée, but it's also easy enough to make for a weeknight dinner. Cook leftover rice in the sauce to soften it up.

SERVES 4

Prep Time: 10 minutes

Cook Time: 20 minutes

4 tablespoons (½ stick) unsalted butter

12 ounces cremini or white button mushrooms, trimmed and sliced

4 to 6 scallions, chopped (about ½ cup)

1 teaspoon kosher salt, divided

2 tablespoons all-purpose flour

¾ cup dry sherry or dry white wine

¾ cup low-sodium vegetable or fish broth

3 tablespoons heavy (whipping) cream

1 tablespoon chopped fresh parsley, divided

2 cups cooked white or brown rice

4 (6-ounce) tilapia fillets

⅛ teaspoon freshly ground black pepper

1. Select Convection Roast and preheat the oven to 325°F.

2. In a large cast-iron or other oven-safe skillet, melt the butter over medium heat until foaming. Sauté the mushrooms and scallions until the mushrooms are soft. Stir in ½ teaspoon of salt and the flour. Cook for 1 minute, stirring constantly. Gradually stir in the sherry. Let the sauce simmer for 3 to 5 minutes, until some of the alcohol evaporates. Add the broth, cream, and 1½ teaspoons of parsley and bring back to a simmer.

3. Stir the rice into the sauce. Place the fish fillets in a single layer on top of the rice and sauce. Sprinkle the fish with the remaining ½ teaspoon of salt and the pepper, then spoon a little of the sauce over the fillets.

4. Roast for 15 to 20 minutes, until the fish flakes with a fork.

5. To serve, spoon some rice onto each plate and top with a fillet. Sprinkle with the remaining 1½ teaspoons of parsley.

SIMPLE SWAP: If you're watching your carbohydrate intake, try substituting chopped cauliflower for the rice. It will cook in the same time as the fish.

COD WITH PESTO AND MIXED ROASTED VEGETABLES

GLUTEN-FREE | ONE-PAN

The vegetables in this dish are reminiscent of ratatouille, but instead of simmering on the stove, they roast in the oven, which browns them and concentrates their flavor. They provide a wonderful complement to a mild white fish like cod, which gets an extra boost of flavor from the pesto.

SERVES 4

Prep Time: 15 minutes, plus
  10 minutes to rest
Cook Time: 20 minutes

1 small eggplant, peeled and
  cut into ½-inch-thick slices

1 small zucchini, cut into
  ½-inch-thick slices

2 teaspoons kosher salt, divided

1 small onion, chopped
  (about 1 cup)

3 garlic cloves, minced

1 small green bell pepper,
  seeded and cut into ½-inch
  chunks (about 1 cup)

1 small red bell pepper, cut into
  ½-inch chunks (about 1 cup)

½ teaspoon dried oregano

¼ teaspoon freshly ground
  black pepper

2 tablespoons extra-virgin olive oil

1 pint cherry tomatoes, halved

4 (6-ounce) cod fillets

⅓ cup pesto, plus more for
  serving (optional)

1. Select Convection Roast and preheat the oven to 375°F.

2. Salt one side of the eggplant and zucchini slices with ¾ teaspoon of salt. Place the slices salted-side down on paper towels. Salt the other sides with another ¾ teaspoon of salt. Let the slices sit for 10 minutes, or until they start to exude water. Rinse and blot dry with more paper towels. Cut the zucchini slices into quarters and the eggplant slices into eighths.

3. Transfer the zucchini and eggplant to a sheet pan and add the onion, garlic, and bell peppers. Drizzle with the oil and sprinkle with the oregano and black pepper, tossing to coat.

4. Roast for 8 minutes. Stir the tomatoes into the vegetable mixture. Place the cod fillets in a single layer on top of the vegetables and sprinkle with the remaining ½ teaspoon of salt. Drizzle the pesto over the fish and vegetables, using a basting brush to spread the pesto evenly over the fillets.

5. Roast for 12 minutes, or until the fish flakes easily with a fork.

6. To serve, spoon the vegetables onto a platter and top with the fish fillets, with additional pesto on the side, if desired.

SIMPLE SWAP: Any mild white fish works well in this dish, such as tilapia, haddock, or snapper.

SNAPPER FILLETS WITH BRAISED CELERY

DAIRY-FREE | GLUTEN-FREE | UNDER 30 MINUTES

This recipe calls for the stalks and leaves of celery, some of which is cooked and some of which is used raw. Once you taste this dish, you'll love celery as much as I do!

SERVES 4

Prep Time: 10 minutes

Cook Time: 15 minutes

4 (6- to 8-ounce) boneless, skinless snapper fillets

1½ teaspoons kosher salt, divided

4 tablespoons extra-virgin olive oil, divided

4 large celery stalks, thinly sliced, divided, leaves reserved and torn

2 garlic cloves, thinly sliced

3 scallions, chopped

⅓ cup low-sodium chicken or vegetable broth

¼ cup dry white wine

½ teaspoon celery seed, divided

1 tablespoon freshly squeezed lemon juice

SIMPLE SWAP: If your celery doesn't have many leaves attached, you can use parsley leaves instead.

1. Select Convection Roast and preheat the oven to 325°F.

2. Sprinkle both sides of each fillet with ¾ teaspoon of salt and set aside.

3. In a 10-inch cast-iron or other oven-safe skillet, heat 2 tablespoons of oil over medium-high heat until shimmering. Add three-quarters of the sliced celery, the garlic, and scallions. Stir-fry for 2 to 3 minutes, until the celery starts to soften. Pour in the broth and wine and bring to a simmer. Stir in ¼ teaspoon of celery seed and ⅜ teaspoon of the remaining salt.

4. Place the fish fillets in a single layer on top of the celery mixture and transfer the skillet to the oven. Roast for 12 to 16 minutes, until the fish flakes with a fork.

5. Meanwhile, put the remaining celery and the celery leaves in a small bowl. In a small jar with a tight lid, combine the remaining 2 tablespoons of oil, lemon juice, remaining ¼ teaspoon of celery seed, and remaining ⅜ teaspoon of salt and shake to combine.

6. When the fish is done, transfer the fillets and braised celery to a platter.

7. Shake the dressing again and pour it over the raw celery and celery leaves, tossing to coat. Top the fish with the celery salad and serve.

THAI-STYLE HALIBUT WITH BOK CHOY

DAIRY-FREE | GLUTEN-FREE | **ONE-PAN** | UNDER 30 MINUTES

Oven braising fish in a fragrant, spicy coconut milk mixture is an easy way to get the great flavors of Thai curry without all the fuss. Flaky, sweet halibut fillets and crisp, peppery baby bok choy pair perfectly in this quick and easy meal. Serve it with rice, if desired.

SERVES 4

Prep Time: 10 minutes

Cook Time: 20 minutes

1 (14-ounce) can coconut milk

2 teaspoons red or green Thai curry paste

1 tablespoon fish sauce

1 tablespoon brown sugar

1 tablespoon freshly squeezed lime juice

6 to 8 baby bok choy, trimmed and halved lengthwise

4 (6- to 8-ounce) halibut fillets

¼ cup chopped fresh cilantro

1. Select Convection Roast and preheat the oven to 400°F.

2. Pour the coconut milk into a 9-by-13-inch baking dish, and put the dish in the oven while it preheats.

3. When the coconut milk just begins to simmer, stir in the curry paste, fish sauce, brown sugar, and lime juice.

4. Place the bok choy halves in a single layer in the baking dish and arrange the halibut fillets on top. Spoon some of the coconut milk mixture over the top of the fish.

5. Roast for about 20 minutes, until the halibut flakes with a fork and the bok choy is tender.

SIMPLE SWAP: If you can't find baby bok choy, you can use a few stalks of regular bok choy. Cut the stems into ½-inch pieces and cut the greens into 1-inch ribbons.

BROILED TUNA STEAKS WITH LEMON-CAPER SAUCE AND ASPARAGUS

DAIRY-FREE | GLUTEN-FREE | UNDER 30 MINUTES

If you don't have a grill, or it's the middle of winter, it's time to turn on the broiler. With a convection setting, tuna steaks achieve a beautifully seared exterior while the interior stays pink and juicy. A side of roasted asparagus completes this elegant yet easy meal.

SERVES 4

Prep Time: 10 minutes

Cook Time: 20 minutes

1 pound asparagus, trimmed

8 tablespoons olive oil, divided

1 teaspoon kosher salt, divided

1 garlic clove, minced

2 tablespoons freshly
squeezed lemon juice

¼ cup chopped fresh
parsley, divided

2 tablespoons drained capers

½ teaspoon freshly ground
black pepper

4 (8-ounce) tuna steaks, about
¾-inch thick

1. Position the top oven rack about 8 inches from the broiling element. Select Convection Roast and preheat the oven to 400°F.

2. Arrange the asparagus on a sheet pan and drizzle with 1 tablespoon of oil. Toss to coat and sprinkle with ½ teaspoon of salt.

3. Roast the asparagus for 7 to 10 minutes depending on thickness, until just barely tender.

4. Meanwhile, in a small saucepan, heat 3 tablespoons of the remaining oil over low heat. Add the garlic and sauté just until fragrant. Stir in the lemon juice, half the parsley, and capers. Remove the pan from the heat and set aside.

5. Remove the sheet pan from the oven and switch the oven to Convection Broil. Select the High setting if possible.

6. Rub the remaining 4 tablespoons of oil over both sides of the tuna steaks, and sprinkle with the remaining ½ teaspoon of salt and the pepper. Place the tuna steaks in a single layer on top of the asparagus. Broil for 8 to 10 minutes, turning the fish carefully about halfway through the cooking time. The tuna steaks should still be pink in the middle, and the asparagus should be tender and browned in spots.

7. To serve, drizzle the warm lemon-caper sauce over the tuna and asparagus, then sprinkle the remaining parsley over the fish.

SIMPLE SWAP: Instead of tuna, try broiling salmon steaks. You may need to decrease the cooking time, depending on the thickness of the steaks.

BARBECUE DRUMSTICKS WITH GREEN BEANS AND SWEET POTATOES page 75

POULTRY

SPICY CHICKEN SANDWICHES WITH ROASTED GARLIC SAUCE

DAIRY-FREE | **UNDER 30 MINUTES**

When you're in the mood for a crispy chicken sandwich without all the grease, turn to this recipe. Panko bread crumbs make the chicken crispy. A creamy roasted garlic sauce mellows the heat of the hot sauce and Cajun seasoning, and it adds a sweet complexity to the sandwich.

SERVES 4

Prep Time: 15 minutes

Cook Time: 15 minutes

5 or 6 large garlic cloves

3 tablespoons extra-virgin olive oil, divided

2 (8- to 10-ounce) boneless, skinless chicken breasts

1 teaspoon kosher salt, divided

1 cup all-purpose flour

1 teaspoon Cajun or Creole seasoning

2 large eggs

½ teaspoon hot sauce

2 cups panko bread crumbs

⅓ cup mayonnaise

4 ciabatta rolls or other sturdy buns, split in half

Lettuce and tomato slices, for serving (optional)

1. Select Convection Roast and preheat the oven to 400°F. Set a rack in a sheet pan.

2. Put the garlic cloves on a piece of aluminum foil and drizzle with 1 tablespoon of oil. Place in the oven while it preheats.

3. Place the chicken breasts on a cutting board and cut each one in half parallel to the board so that you have four flat fillets. Place a piece of plastic wrap over the chicken pieces and use a rolling pin or small skillet to gently pound them to an even thickness of about ½ inch. Season the chicken on both sides with ½ teaspoon of salt.

4. In a shallow bowl, mix the flour, remaining ½ teaspoon of salt, and the Cajun seasoning. In another shallow bowl, whisk together the eggs and hot sauce. In a third shallow bowl, combine the panko and remaining 2 tablespoons of oil.

5. Lightly dredge both sides of the chicken pieces in the seasoned flour, then dip them in the egg wash to coat completely, letting the excess drip off. Finally, dredge the chicken in the panko. Carefully place the breaded chicken pieces on the prepared rack.

6. Roast the chicken for 7 to 8 minutes, then carefully turn the pieces over. Return the pan to the oven and roast for another 5 to 6 minutes, until the chicken is no longer pink in the center.

7. Let the chicken rest while you make the sauce. Put the mayonnaise in a small bowl. Remove the packet of garlic from the oven and smash it before adding it to the mayonnaise. Smash the garlic and stir to combine.

8. Divide the sauce among the bun bottoms and top each with a piece of chicken. Add lettuce and tomato slices (if using) and close the buns.

SIMPLE SWAP: If you're not a garlic fan, mix the mayonnaise with a teaspoon of Dijon mustard instead.

CRISPY GARLIC CHICKEN THIGHS WITH POTATOES AND CARROTS

DAIRY-FREE | GLUTEN-FREE | ONE-PAN

This dish hits all the right notes for a stellar one-pan supper: crispy chicken skin, roasted vegetables, tangy lemon, and mellow garlic. For a variation, try roasting the chicken with your favorite root vegetables or with Brussels sprouts.

SERVES 4

Prep Time: 10 minutes

Cook Time: 40 minutes

¼ cup olive oil

2 pounds bone-in, skin-on chicken thighs

1½ teaspoons kosher salt, divided

1 small lemon

20 garlic cloves, (about ½ cup)

12 ounces small red potatoes (about 2 inches in diameter), quartered

2 large carrots, peeled and cut into 1-inch pieces

⅓ cup low-sodium chicken broth

½ teaspoon freshly ground black pepper

1. Select Convection Roast and preheat the oven to 425°F. Coat a sheet pan with the oil and place in the oven while it preheats.

2. Salt the chicken thighs on both sides with ¾ teaspoon of salt.

3. When the oven is heated, remove the sheet pan and place the chicken thighs skin-side down on it. Roast the chicken for 10 minutes.

4. Meanwhile, cut the ends off the lemon and use a mandoline or knife to slice it very thin. Cut the slices in half and remove any seeds.

5. Transfer the chicken thighs to a cutting board or plate. Put the garlic cloves, carrots, and potatoes on the sheet pan and sprinkle with the remaining ¾ teaspoon of salt. Toss to coat with the oil, then move the vegetables to the outer edges of the pan. Arrange the lemon slices in the center of the pan in two or three layers and place the chicken thighs on top of them, skin-side up.

6. Roast for 30 to 35 minutes, until the chicken registers 175°F and the carrots and potatoes are golden brown and crisp.

7. Transfer the chicken, carrots, and potatoes to a platter. Add the chicken broth and pepper to the sheet pan and mix with the chicken juices, smashing the garlic slightly as you stir. Pour the sauce around the chicken and vegetables and serve.

FOR COUNTERTOP OVENS: With a smaller sheet pan, you will probably have to move some of the potatoes and garlic under the chicken so everything fits. Your potatoes won't get as crisp, but the dish will be just as tasty. Alternately, skip the potatoes and serve with crusty bread to sop up the sauce.

EVEN EASIER: Buy bags or jars of peeled garlic cloves at the grocery store to cut way down on prep time.

TERIYAKI CHICKEN WITH SNOW PEAS

DAIRY-FREE | GLUTEN-FREE

In America, we tend to think of teriyaki as a sauce. But in Japan, teriyaki refers to a method of cooking meat—it's soaked in a marinade or glazed, then grilled or broiled. Try serving this teriyaki chicken with white or brown rice.

SERVES 4

Prep Time: 10 minutes, plus
*   30 minutes to marinate*
Cook Time: 20 minutes

½ cup tamari or other
   gluten-free soy sauce

3 tablespoons honey

1 tablespoon rice vinegar

1 tablespoon rice wine or
   dry sherry

2 teaspoons minced
   fresh ginger

2 garlic cloves, minced

1½ pounds boneless, skinless
   chicken thighs

2 teaspoons toasted sesame oil

8 to 12 ounces snow peas

EVEN EASIER: Use a
commercial teriyaki sauce
instead of making your own.

1. Select Convection Roast and preheat the oven to 400°F.

2. In a small bowl, whisk together the tamari, honey, vinegar, rice wine, ginger, and garlic until the honey is dissolved. Set aside 2 tablespoons of the marinade and pour the rest into a zip-top bag. Put the chicken thighs in the bag and seal, squeezing as much air out as possible. Squish the chicken around to coat it completely, then let the chicken marinate for 30 minutes, turning the bag every 10 minutes.

3. Put the snow peas on a sheet pan and toss with the reserved marinade and the oil. Move the peas to the outer edges of the pan.

4. Arrange the chicken in a single layer in the center of the pan.

5. Roast the chicken and peas for 8 minutes. Remove from the oven. Turn the chicken over and stir the peas. Roast for another 10 minutes, or until the chicken is browning in spots and the peas are tender.

FOR COUNTERTOP OVENS: You'll probably need to place the chicken on top of the snow peas. They'll cook fine but won't get as browned.

ADOBO-STYLE CHICKEN AND RICE

DAIRY-FREE | GLUTEN-FREE | ONE-PAN

Think of this dish as a cross between chicken adobo and arroz con pollo. The chicken marinates in vinegar, soy sauce, and spices like chicken adobo, then rice and liquid are added to the pot, and the dish is finished in the oven. One pot, no fuss.

SERVES 4

Prep Time: 10 minutes, plus
1 hour to marinate

Cook Time: 30 minutes

½ cup white vinegar

¼ cup tamari or other
gluten-free soy sauce

6 garlic cloves, lightly smashed

1 teaspoon coarsely ground
black pepper

2 dried bay leaves

2 pounds boneless, skinless
chicken thighs

1 cup long-grain white rice

1¼ cups water

½ cup low-sodium chicken broth

1. In a Dutch oven or other oven-safe pot, combine the vinegar, tamari, garlic, pepper, and bay leaves. Add the chicken, cover, and marinate in the refrigerator for 1 to 3 hours.

2. Select Convection Roast and preheat the oven to 350°F.

3. Add the rice, water, and broth to the pot with the chicken, lifting the chicken pieces up so the rice sinks to the bottom. Place the pot over medium heat and bring the liquid to a simmer.

4. Cover the pot and place it in the oven. Bake for 20 minutes, then stir. The rice should be barely tender, with some liquid remaining in the pot. Return the pot to the oven uncovered, and bake for another 10 minutes or so, until the rice is tender and the chicken is done (cut into the thickest part to be sure no pink remains). Remove the bay leaves and garlic.

5. Spoon the rice onto plates and top with the chicken.

HELPFUL HACK: If you use boiling water, you can skip heating the dish on the stovetop.

CHICKEN TENDERS WITH SPINACH-ARTICHOKE GRATIN

GLUTEN-FREE | ONE-PAN

It isn't difficult to turn spinach and artichoke dip into a main dish. This recipe tops the vegetables with chicken tenders. To cut this dish's richness, try serving it with a tomato and cucumber salad with a tangy vinaigrette.

SERVES 4

Prep Time: 10 minutes

Cook Time: 25 minutes

1½ pounds chicken tenders (see Helpful Hack tip)

1 teaspoon kosher salt, divided

2 tablespoons unsalted butter

1 small onion, chopped

3 garlic cloves, minced

1 pound baby spinach

1 (14-ounce) can artichoke hearts, drained

½ cup heavy (whipping) cream

4 ounces cream cheese, softened

¼ cup grated Parmesan cheese

1 cup shredded mozzarella cheese

1. Select Convection Roast and preheat the oven to 350°F.

2. Sprinkle the chicken with ½ teaspoon of salt and set aside.

3. In a large cast-iron or other oven-safe skillet, melt the butter over medium heat. When the butter is foaming, add the onion, sprinkle with the remaining ½ teaspoon of salt, and cook, stirring, for 1 to 2 minutes, until the onion starts to soften. Add the garlic and stir for about 30 seconds. Add the spinach in large handfuls, stirring to wilt. Add the artichoke hearts, stirring them into the spinach. Add the heavy cream and cream cheese and cook until the cream cheese has melted into the vegetables. Stir in the Parmesan.

4. Pat the chicken dry and arrange the tenders in a single layer on top of the spinach mixture. Top with the mozzarella cheese.

5. Put the skillet in the oven and bake for 35 to 40 minutes, until the cheese is lightly browned on top and the mixture is bubbling.

6. Let cool for 5 to 10 minutes, then serve.

HELPFUL HACK: A chicken "tender" is the piece of breast meat that runs along a boned breast half. They used to be common in the meat case but can be hard to find these days. If you can't find them, just cut boneless, skinless breasts into 1-inch-thick strips.

EVEN EASIER: Use frozen spinach, thawed and well drained, in place of the fresh spinach.

EASY CHICKEN POT PIE

ONE-PAN

I've made chicken pot pies according to some pretty exhausting instructions. Bottom crust baked separately, filled with chicken and vegetables cooked separately, combined with a sauce that is also—you guessed it!—cooked separately, and finished with yet another crust. I'll let you in on a secret: You can make a pretty tasty pot pie without all that fuss.

SERVES 4

Prep Time: 10 minutes

Cook Time: 30 minutes

4 tablespoons (½ stick) unsalted butter

½ cup chopped onion

¼ cup all-purpose flour

½ teaspoon kosher salt

¼ teaspoon freshly ground black pepper

1¾ cups low-sodium chicken broth

½ cup whole milk

2½ cups shredded cooked chicken

2 cups frozen mixed vegetables, thawed

1 (9-inch) refrigerated piecrust

1. Select Convection Bake and preheat the oven to 425°F.

2. In a large cast-iron skillet, melt the butter over medium heat. Add the onion and cook, stirring, until softened. Stir in the flour, salt, and pepper until well blended. Gradually stir in the broth and milk, and cook, stirring occasionally, until bubbly and thickened, about 5 minutes.

3. Stir in the chicken and mixed vegetables. Remove from the heat. Top with the crust, pressing the dough over the edges of the skillet to seal. Cut 3 or 4 slits into the crust.

4. Put the skillet in the oven and bake for 30 to 40 minutes, until the crust is golden brown and the filling is bubbling. Let stand for 5 minutes before serving.

SIMPLE SWAP: Use puff pastry instead of pie dough for the crust.

BARBECUE DRUMSTICKS WITH GREEN BEANS AND SWEET POTATOES

DAIRY-FREE | GLUTEN-FREE | ONE-PAN

Commercial barbecue sauce makes this sheet-pan meal a breeze to prepare.

SERVES 4

Prep Time: 10 minutes

Cook Time: 25 minutes

8 chicken drumsticks

1 teaspoon kosher salt, divided

1 pound sweet potatoes, peeled and cut into 1-inch chunks

3 tablespoons vegetable oil, divided

1 cup barbecue sauce (I like KC Masterpiece), plus more if desired

8 ounces green beans, trimmed

1. Select Convection Roast and preheat the oven to 375°F.

2. Season the drumsticks on all sides with ½ teaspoon of salt. Let sit for a few minutes, then blot dry with a paper towel.

3. Put the sweet potato chunks on a sheet pan and drizzle with 2 tablespoons of oil. Move them to one side of the pan.

4. Place the drumsticks on the other side of the pan. Brush all sides of the chicken with half the barbecue sauce.

5. Roast for 15 minutes. Brush the drumsticks with the remaining barbecue sauce. Add the beans to the sweet potatoes and drizzle with the remaining 1 tablespoon of oil. Add the remaining ½ teaspoon of salt, and toss the beans and potatoes together. Roast for another 15 to 20 minutes, until the vegetables are sizzling and browned in spots and the chicken is cooked through.

6. If you like, brush the drumsticks with additional barbecue sauce, and serve with the beans and sweet potatoes on the side.

FOR COUNTERTOP OVENS: Because your sheet pan will be smaller, you'll be unable to arrange the sweet potatoes in a single layer. To accommodate a smaller pan, cut the potatoes slightly smaller, and stir them several times for more even cooking.

UPSIDE-DOWN CHICKEN NACHOS

GLUTEN-FREE | ONE-PAN

The problem with loaded nachos is that the chips start to get soggy and limp. Why not put the toppings on the bottom? I'm sure I'm not the only person to think of this, but I'm still taking credit.

SERVES 4

Prep Time: 10 minutes

Cook Time: 30 minutes

1½ pounds boneless, skinless chicken thighs

1 teaspoon kosher salt

1¼ cups tomato-based salsa

1 (14-ounce) can pinto beans, rinsed and drained

8 ounces Monterey Jack cheese, shredded

4 ounces tortilla chips, or more as needed

1 medium jalapeño pepper, seeded and minced, or ¼ cup sliced pickled jalapeños (optional)

1. Select Convection Roast and preheat the oven to 350°F.

2. Season the chicken thighs on both sides with the salt, and place the thighs in a single layer in a 9-by-13-inch baking dish. Pour about ⅔ cup of salsa over the chicken. Place the pan in the oven and bake for 20 to 25 minutes, until the chicken is nearly done (if the thickest parts aren't quite done, it's okay—the chicken will cook again).

3. Remove the chicken from the dish and chop or pull the meat into ½-inch pieces, discarding any gristle or fat.

4. Pour the beans into the dish and smash lightly with a potato masher or large fork so they are broken up but not smooth. Return the chicken to the pan, add the remaining salsa, and stir to combine.

5. Increase the oven temperature to 400°F and place the dish in the oven—don't wait for the temperature to rise. Cook the chicken and beans for 7 to 8 minutes, until bubbling.

6. Sprinkle about one-quarter of the cheese over the chicken mixture. Arrange the tortilla chips over the chicken in an even layer, covering the chicken mixture but not overlapping the chips too much. Sprinkle the remaining cheese over the chips, then top with the jalapeño (if using).

7. Return to the oven and bake for 5 to 7 minutes, until the cheese is melted and the chips are beginning to brown on the edges.

8. Serve immediately, scooping the chicken and beans out with the chips.

SIMPLE SWAP: Substitute cooked ground beef instead of the chicken, skipping steps 2 and 3.

EASY CHICKEN CORDON BLEU

GLUTEN-FREE OPTION

Classic chicken cordon bleu is wonderful—when someone else makes it. It's delicious but time-consuming and messy. Instead of butterflying, stuffing, dredging, and frying the chicken, in this recipe you layer it with prosciutto and cheese. A buttery, cheese-laced crumb topping provides satisfying crunch. Serve this dish with a tossed green salad for a complete dinner.

SERVES 4

Prep Time: 15 minutes

Cook Time: 35 minutes

Nonstick cooking spray

2 (10- to 12-ounce) boneless, skinless chicken breasts

½ teaspoon kosher salt

4 teaspoons Dijon mustard

4 thin slices prosciutto

4 thin slices Gruyère, Emmental, or other Swiss-style cheese

⅔ cup panko bread crumbs (gluten-free if necessary)

2 tablespoons unsalted butter, melted

¼ cup grated Parmesan cheese

1. Select Convection Roast and preheat the oven to 375°F. Spray a 9-by-13-inch baking dish with cooking spray.

2. Lay the chicken breasts flat on a cutting board. With your knife parallel to the board, slice each breast across, for a total of four flat pieces. Sprinkle the chicken with the salt. Lay a piece of plastic wrap over the chicken pieces, and use the heel of your hand to press the chicken into a more even thickness.

3. Transfer the chicken pieces to the prepared baking dish. Spread 1 teaspoon of mustard on each chicken piece. Layer one slice of ham and one slice of cheese evenly over each chicken piece.

4. In a small bowl, mix together the bread crumbs, melted butter, and Parmesan cheese. Sprinkle the mixture over the top of each piece.

5. Bake for 30 to 35 minutes, until the topping is browned and the chicken is done—slide a paring knife into one of the chicken pieces to be sure.

SIMPLE SWAP: If you don't have prosciutto, you can use regular baked or boiled ham.

HONEY-GLAZED TURKEY TENDERLOINS WITH CARROTS AND SNAP PEAS

DAIRY-FREE | GLUTEN-FREE

Turkey tenderloins are boneless strips of breast meat. If you get them pre-brined, they are injected with a salt solution, so don't salt them.

SERVES 4

Prep Time: 10 minutes

Cook Time: 25 minutes

2 (12-ounce) turkey tenderloins

1 teaspoon kosher salt, divided

3 tablespoons balsamic vinegar

2 tablespoons honey

1 tablespoon Dijon mustard

½ teaspoon dried thyme

6 large carrots, peeled and cut into ¼-inch-thick slices

8 ounces snap peas

1 tablespoon extra-virgin olive oil

SIMPLE SWAP: You can make this dish with pork tenderloin in place of the turkey. Cook the pork until it reaches 145°F in the center.

1. Select Convection Roast and preheat the oven to 375°F.

2. If your turkey tenderloins are not pre-brined, sprinkle them with ¾ teaspoon of salt. Place the turkey on a sheet pan.

3. In a small bowl, mix the balsamic vinegar, honey, mustard, and thyme.

4. Put the carrots and snap peas in a medium bowl and drizzle with the oil. Add 1 tablespoon of the balsamic mixture and the remaining ¼ teaspoon of salt, and toss to coat. Scatter the vegetables on the pan around the turkey tenderloins. Brush the tenderloins with about half of the remaining balsamic mixture.

5. Roast the turkey and vegetables for 10 to 12 minutes, then remove the pan from the oven. Gently stir the vegetables. Flip the tenderloins and baste them with the remaining balsamic mixture. Cook for another 10 to 15 minutes, until the center of the tenderloins registers 155°F on a meat thermometer.

6. Slice the turkey and serve with the vegetables.

FOR COUNTERTOP OVENS: On a smaller sheet pan, you'll need to place the turkey on top of some of the vegetables, but this won't affect the cooking time. Stir the vegetables more often to ensure even cooking.

TURKEY BREAST WITH HERB BUTTER AND CORNBREAD DRESSING

ONE-PAN

For a small Thanksgiving dinner, or anytime you want to pretend it's a holiday, a turkey breast is a great choice. You can always roast it whole, but it will cook more evenly if split in two along the breastbone. Starting the dressing in an oven-safe skillet allows you to cook the whole dish in one pan.

SERVES 4

Prep Time: 15 minutes

Cook Time: 40 minutes

1 (4- to 5-pound) bone-in turkey breast, split at the breastbone

2½ teaspoons kosher salt, divided

6 tablespoons (¾ stick) unsalted butter, softened, divided

½ small onion, finely chopped

1 celery stalk, finely chopped

½ teaspoon freshly ground black pepper, divided

2 tablespoons finely chopped fresh sage, divided

2 teaspoons finely chopped fresh thyme, divided

¾ cup chicken broth

4 cups stale cornbread, crumbled into large pieces

1 large egg, beaten

1. Select Convection Roast and preheat the oven to 400°F.

2. Sprinkle the turkey breast halves with 1¼ teaspoons of salt. Let it rest while you make the dressing.

3. In a large, oven-safe skillet, melt 3 tablespoons of butter over medium-high heat. Add the onion, celery, remaining 1¼ teaspoons of salt, and ¼ teaspoon of pepper and sauté until the vegetables soften, 5 to 6 minutes. Stir in 1 tablespoon of sage, 1 teaspoon of thyme, and the chicken broth and simmer, uncovered, until the liquid is reduced by about a third, about 3 minutes. Add the cornbread and toss to mix. Stir in the egg.

4. In a small bowl, mix the remaining 3 tablespoons of butter with the remaining 1 tablespoon of sage, 1 teaspoon of thyme, and ¼ teaspoon of pepper. With your fingers, loosen the skin over the turkey breast meat. Scoop half the butter mixture under the skin on each breast half and spread it around with your hands as evenly as possible. Place the turkey breast halves on top of the dressing in the skillet.

5. Transfer the skillet to the oven and roast until a meat thermometer inserted into the turkey reaches 160°F, 35 to 45 minutes. Remove the skillet from the oven and let the turkey rest for 5 to 10 minutes before carving. Serve the turkey with the dressing.

EVEN EASIER: Use a stuffing mix instead of making your own. Just follow the package directions.

ROASTED DUCK BREASTS WITH OVEN FRIES

DAIRY-FREE | GLUTEN-FREE | ONE-PAN

Duck breasts are richer and moister than chicken breasts, and their flavor is more like that of dark meat. You'll likely find white Pekin (a.k.a. Long Island), Muscovy, or Moulard duck at your supermarket. Pekin and Muscovy breasts are small—about 8 ounces each—whereas Moulard breasts (known as magrets) weigh about 1 pound.

SERVES 4

Prep Time: 10 minutes

Cook Time: 25 minutes

4 (8-ounce) or 2 (1-pound) boneless, skin-on duck breast halves

2 teaspoons kosher salt

1 pound russet potatoes, peeled and cut into very thin sticks

1. Select Convection Roast and preheat the oven to 400°F. Place a sheet pan in the oven as it heats.

2. With a very sharp knife, gently score the skin side of each duck breast, cutting through the skin and fat but not into the flesh. Space the scores ¼ to ½ inch apart. Turn the breast 90 degrees and score at right angles to the first series of scores. You'll have a diamond pattern of cuts over the skin. Sprinkle both sides with 1 teaspoon of salt.

3. When the oven is up to temperature, take the pan out and arrange the breasts on it, skin-side down. Roast until the skin is light brown and beginning to crisp and most of the fat has rendered, about 4 minutes.

4. Remove the pan from the oven and arrange the potatoes around the breasts. Toss them to coat with the rendered duck fat and sprinkle with the remaining 1 teaspoon of salt. Roast for another 3 to 4 minutes, until the duck skin is dark golden brown.

5. Turn the breasts over and toss the potatoes. Continue to roast until the duck reaches an internal temperature of 150°F. This can take anywhere from 4 to 8 minutes, depending on the type of duck and the size of the breasts.

6. Remove the pan from the oven and let it rest for 5 minutes before slicing the duck. Serve with the fries.

EVEN EASIER: Use frozen French fries instead of starting with raw potatoes. Follow the package directions for the cooking time, but coat them in the rendered duck fat for best results.

LAMB CURRY page 104

BEEF, PORK, AND LAMB

CHINESE-STYLE PEPPER STEAK "STIR-FRY"

DAIRY-FREE | GLUTEN-FREE | **ONE-PAN** | UNDER 30 MINUTES

No, this dish is not a true stir-fry; it's an oven braise. But it approximates the flavor profile of the Chinese-American restaurant favorite pepper steak. The dish's heavy use of ground black pepper was inspired by Kenji López-Alt's recipe at the website Serious Eats. Serve the dish as is or over white or brown rice.

SERVES 4

Prep Time: 10 minutes

Cook Time: 15 minutes

1 pound sirloin, flat iron, or flank steak, cut into ¼-inch-thick strips

1 teaspoon kosher salt

¼ cup low-sodium beef or chicken broth

¼ cup dry sherry or rice wine

3 tablespoons tamari or other gluten-free soy sauce

3 tablespoons rice vinegar

1 tablespoon toasted sesame oil

1 tablespoon vegetable oil

1 tablespoon sugar

2 teaspoons minced garlic

2 teaspoons minced ginger

1½ teaspoons freshly ground black pepper

1 teaspoon cornstarch

1. Select Convection Roast and preheat the oven to 375°F.

2. Season the beef slices on all sides with the salt and set aside.

3. In a 9-by-13-inch baking dish, combine the broth, sherry, tamari, vinegar, sesame oil, vegetable oil, sugar, garlic, ginger, black pepper, and cornstarch. Stir to combine.

4. Add the peppers and onion to the baking dish, and toss to coat with the sauce.

1 medium red bell pepper, cut into bite-size pieces

1 medium green bell pepper, cut into bite-size pieces

1 small onion, cut into ¼-inch-thick wedges

2 scallions, thinly sliced

5. Roast the vegetables for 6 minutes, or until they're just becoming tender. Add the beef and toss to combine it with the vegetables. Roast for 10 minutes, or until the beef is just cooked through.

6. Serve, garnished with the scallions.

EVEN EASIER: If you can find Dorot brand frozen ginger cubes (Trader Joe's carries them), they're very good and much easier than mincing your own fresh ginger.

ITALIAN-STYLE MEATLOAF

Say goodbye to meatloaf smothered with sauce to make up for a dry texture. A convection oven makes this meatloaf's texture perfect, inside and out.

SERVES 4

Prep Time: 15 minutes

Cook Time: 1 hour

1 large egg

¼ cup whole milk

24 saltines, crushed but not pulverized

1 pound ground chuck

1 pound Italian sausage, casing removed

¼ cup grated Parmesan cheese

1 teaspoon kosher salt

1 cup marinara sauce, plus more for serving (optional)

¾ cup shredded mozzarella cheese

1. Select Convection Roast and preheat the oven to 350°F. Line a sheet pan with aluminum foil.

2. In a large bowl, whisk the egg into the milk, then stir in the crackers. Let sit for 5 minutes to hydrate.

3. With your hands, crumble the ground chuck and sausage into the milk mixture, alternating beef and sausage. When you've added about half the meat, sprinkle about half the grated Parmesan and half the salt over the mixture. Continue breaking up the meat until it's all in the bowl, then add the remaining Parmesan and salt. Gently mix everything together well, but try not to overwork the meat.

4. Form the meat mixture into a loaf shape and transfer the meatloaf to the prepared sheet pan.

5. Bake for 30 minutes, then rotate the pan. Bake for another 20 minutes, then check the temperature. The meatloaf should be 160°F. Cook for another 10 to 20 minutes to reach the desired temperature.

6. When the meatloaf reaches 160°F, increase the oven temperature to 400°F. Spread the marinara sauce over the top of the meatloaf and sprinkle with the mozzarella. When the oven is up to temperature, return the meatloaf to the oven and bake until the cheese is bubbling and lightly browned, 6 to 8 minutes.

7. Let the meatloaf cool for 15 to 20 minutes to firm it up. Slice and serve with additional marinara (warmed), if you like.

HELPFUL HACK: If you have a standard loaf pan, you can line it with plastic wrap and form the meatloaf in it. Make it a little higher than you think it should be, because it will slump a bit in the oven. Transfer the loaf to the sheet pan and remove the plastic wrap.

SIMPLE SWAP: My partner, Dave, is not fond of tomato sauce on meatloaf, so I usually omit the marinara and mozzarella. Instead, I sprinkle on a thin layer of grated Parmesan in step 6 and bake just until brown and crunchy.

SLOW-ROASTED SALT AND PEPPER BEEF RIBS

DAIRY-FREE | GLUTEN-FREE | ONE-PAN

Beef back ribs are the "rack" from a standing rib roast. If you frequent a market that carries boneless rib roasts, you have access to racks of beef back ribs, although you may need to ask for them. If all you see in the case are bone-in roasts, ask the butcher to cut the ribs off one of them. Unlike the roast to which they are attached, the ribs are better when they're cooked to at least medium doneness.

SERVES 4

Prep Time: 10 minutes

Cook Time: 3 hours

2 racks beef back ribs (3 to 6 ribs each, for a total of at least 8 ribs)

Kosher salt

Freshly ground black pepper

1. Select Convection Roast and preheat the oven to 350°F. Line a sheet pan with aluminum foil and set a rack on the pan.

2. Place the ribs on the rack, meaty-side up, and roast for 20 minutes. Flip and rotate the ribs. Reduce the oven temperature to 225°F and put the pan back in immediately—no need to wait for the oven temperature to adapt.

3. Roast for 2½ to 3 more hours, flipping and rotating the ribs every 40 minutes. The ribs are done when the racks are flexible and the meat has drawn back from the ends of the bones by about ¾ inch.

4. Slice the racks into individual ribs, season with salt and pepper, and serve.

SIMPLE SWAP: The ribs are awesome with just salt and pepper, but don't be shy about adding a glaze in the last few minutes of cooking, if that's the way you roll. The mustard glaze from the Slow-Roasted Spareribs (page 96) is nice, as is a mix of hot sauce and honey.

CLASSIC POT ROAST

DAIRY-FREE | GLUTEN-FREE | ONE-PAN

For best results, choose a flat piece of chuck roast that is 2½ to 3 inches thick. Cook the beef most of the way before adding the vegetables to keep them from turning to mush.

SERVES 4

Prep Time: 15 minutes

Cook Time: 2 hours

1 (2½-pound) beef chuck (shoulder) roast

1 teaspoon kosher salt

½ teaspoon freshly ground black pepper

1 tablespoon vegetable oil

2 tablespoons tomato paste

½ cup dry red wine

2 cups low-sodium beef broth

1 teaspoon Worcestershire sauce

8 ounces boiling onions (about 2 inches in diameter)

4 large carrots, peeled and cut into 2-inch pieces

1 pound small red or Yukon Gold potatoes (1 to 2 inches in diameter)

1. Select Convection Roast and preheat the oven to 300°F.

2. Season the roast on all sides with the salt and pepper.

3. Heat the oil in a large Dutch oven over medium heat until it shimmers. Brown the roast on all sides, about 8 minutes total. Transfer the roast to a plate. Add the tomato paste to the pot and cook, stirring, until the paste has darkened slightly, about 1 minute. Add the red wine and bring to a simmer, scraping up the browned bits. Stir in the beef broth and Worcestershire sauce. Place the roast in the liquid.

4. Cover and place the pot in the oven. Bake for 60 to 90 minutes, until the roast is barely tender.

5. Add the onions, carrots, and potatoes and return the pot to the oven, uncovered. Bake for another 30 to 40 minutes, until the vegetables are tender and the beef pulls apart easily with a fork.

6. To serve, slice the beef and place on a platter, surrounded with the vegetables. Pour the sauce over the top.

SIMPLE SWAP: Try this recipe with a piece of boneless lamb shoulder.

BEEF RIB ROAST

DAIRY-FREE | GLUTEN-FREE | ONE-PAN

There's nothing quite like a standing rib roast for a show-stopping entrée. A convection oven makes it easy to get perfect results—low, even heat cooks the roast through, and the blast of heat at the end results in a nicely browned crust.

SERVES 4

Prep Time: 5 minutes,
*   plus 1 day to rest*
Cook Time: 3 hours,
*   plus 1 hour to rest*

Kosher salt (about ½ teaspoon per pound of meat)

Freshly ground black pepper (about ¼ teaspoon per pound of meat)

1 bone-in rib roast (3 or 4 ribs)

1. Line a sheet pan with paper towels and set a rack on it.

2. Mix the salt and pepper together and rub it all over the roast. Place the roast on the prepared rack and pan, tent it very loosely with aluminum foil, and refrigerate for at least 1 and up to 4 days.

3. Set the oven rack in the lower middle position. Select Convection Roast and preheat the oven to 225°F.

4. Remove the roast from the refrigerator. Examine the roast for dry spots on either the meat or fat, and trim them off. Remove the paper towels from the sheet pan and set the roast back on the rack, fat-side up. Roast to an internal temperature of 130°F for medium-rare. This will take about 3 hours, but start checking the temperature at 2½ hours.

5. When the desired internal temperature has been reached, remove the roast from the oven and let it rest for 30 to 60 minutes.

6. Turn the oven temperature to 500°F. Ten minutes before serving, put the roast back in the oven for about 7 minutes (checking at 5 minutes) to brown and crisp the crust. Carve and serve immediately.

FOR COUNTERTOP OVENS: Depending on the size of your roast, you may not be able to fit it in a countertop oven with the bones in, so a boneless roast is probably a better choice. Place it on a rack on its side to roast. When you're browning it at the end, turn it over halfway through to brown both sides evenly.

OVEN GOULASH

DAIRY-FREE OPTION | GLUTEN-FREE | ONE-PAN

Authentic Hungarian goulash is a hearty beef stew flavored with sweet paprika. This version includes sausage and plenty of vegetables. Serve it with crusty bread to soak up the sauce.

SERVES 4

Prep Time: 10 minutes

Cook Time: 2 hours

1 pound beef chuck roast, trimmed and cut into 1½-inch pieces

1 teaspoon kosher salt, divided

2 tablespoons vegetable oil, divided

2 medium onions, sliced

2 garlic cloves, minced

¼ cup paprika

2 teaspoons caraway seeds

2 teaspoons dried marjoram or oregano

3 cups low-sodium beef broth

1 (14-ounce) can diced tomatoes, drained

12 ounces kielbasa or other smoked sausage, cut into 1-inch pieces

1. Select Convection Roast and preheat the oven to 350°F.

2. Sprinkle the beef with ½ teaspoon of salt. In a Dutch oven, heat 1 tablespoon of oil over medium heat until shimmering. Working in batches, add the pieces of beef and sear them on two sides, then transfer to a bowl. Add the remaining 1 tablespoon of oil to the pot, then add the onions and garlic and sprinkle with the remaining ½ teaspoon of salt. Cook, stirring, until the onions and garlic have softened, about 3 minutes. Add the paprika, caraway, and marjoram and stir to coat the onions. Cook for about 1 minute or until the spices are fragrant.

3. Pour in the beef broth and stir to dissolve the spices. Return the beef to the pot, along with the tomatoes, and bring the mixture to a simmer.

2 large carrots, peeled and cut into 1-inch pieces

2 medium red bell peppers, cut into 1-inch pieces

8 ounces small red potatoes, quartered

⅓ cup sour cream (optional)

4. Cover and place in the oven. Bake for 60 to 90 minutes, until the meat is just tender.

5. Add the sausage, carrots, bell peppers, and potatoes. Cover and bake for 30 minutes, or until the vegetables are tender.

6. Stir in the sour cream (if using) and serve.

SIMPLE SWAP: For a more traditional Hungarian goulash, increase the beef to 1¾ pounds and omit the sausage. Mix 1 tablespoon of all-purpose flour into the broth before adding the meat, and omit the sour cream.

SLOW-ROASTED SPARERIBS WITH MUSTARD BARBECUE SAUCE

DAIRY-FREE | GLUTEN-FREE OPTION

Look for St. Louis–style ribs, which are trimmed to make them easier to cut. If you like, you can score or remove the membrane that covers the bone side of the ribs. Some people find it tough, although it gets more tender with cooking.

SERVES 4

Prep Time: 10 minutes

Cook Time: 3 hours

1 large rack spareribs

1 teaspoon kosher salt

¼ cup yellow mustard

¼ cup Dijon mustard

2 tablespoons honey

1 tablespoon ketchup
    (gluten-free if desired)

2 teaspoons
    Worcestershire sauce

1 teaspoon freshly ground
    black pepper

1. Select Convection Roast and preheat the oven to 250°F. Line a sheet pan with aluminum foil and set a rack in it.

2. Season the ribs on both sides with the salt and place it on the prepared rack and pan.

3. Roast the ribs for 20 minutes. Flip and rotate the ribs, then return them to the oven. Reduce the oven temperature to 225°F.

4. Roast for 2½ to 3 more hours, flipping and rotating every 40 minutes. The ribs are done when the rack of ribs is flexible and the meat has drawn back from the ends of the bones by about ¾ inch.

5. When the ribs are nearly done, make the sauce. In a small saucepan, stir together the mustards, honey, ketchup, Worcestershire sauce, and pepper. Bring to a simmer over medium heat and cook, stirring occasionally, for 15 to 20 minutes, until slightly thickened.

6. When the ribs are done, baste them on the meaty side with some of the mustard sauce and return them to the oven for 5 to 10 minutes to set the sauce.

7. Slice into individual ribs and serve with the remaining sauce.

FOR COUNTERTOP OVENS: You will probably need to cut the rack of ribs in half, but this will not affect the cooking time.

EVEN EASIER: If you use a commercial barbecue sauce, you can save both time and a dirty saucepan.

BACON-WRAPPED PORK TENDERLOIN WITH APPLES

DAIRY-FREE | GLUTEN-FREE

Pork and apples are a classic combination, as in this recipe for tenderloin with roasted apples and onions. Because tenderloin is so lean, wrapping it in bacon helps keep it moist and gives it a great smoky flavor.

SERVES 4

Prep Time: 10 minutes

Cook Time: 25 minutes

1 (1- to 1¼-pound)
   pork tenderloin

1 teaspoon kosher salt, divided

4 to 6 bacon slices
   (not thick-cut)

2 tablespoons apple
   cider vinegar

2 tablespoons honey

1 tablespoon Dijon mustard

1 tablespoon olive oil

½ teaspoon dried thyme

1 large apple, peeled,
   cored, and cut into
   ¼-inch-thick slices

1 medium onion, cut into
   ¼-inch-thick slices

SIMPLE SWAP: Try using turkey tenderloin instead of pork. The timing will be the same; just be sure the interior of the meat reaches 155°F.

1. Select Convection Roast and preheat the oven to 375°F.

2. Sprinkle the pork all over with ¾ teaspoon of salt (if your tenderloin is brined, omit this step). Wrap the tenderloin with the bacon slices, securing the bacon with toothpicks if necessary.

3. In a small bowl, mix together the vinegar, honey, mustard, oil, and thyme.

4. Put the apple and onion slices on a sheet pan. Drizzle with half the honey mixture and toss to coat. Move the apples and onions to the outer edges of the pan. Place the pork in the center of the pan and baste it with about half the remaining honey mixture and sprinkle with the remaining ¼ teaspoon of salt.

5. Roast for 12 minutes. Stir the apples and onions. Turn the tenderloin over and baste with the remaining honey mixture.

6. Return the pan to the oven and roast for another 12 to 15 minutes, until the apples are soft and the interior of the pork registers between 140°F and 145°F.

BRAISED BRATWURST AND CABBAGE

DAIRY-FREE | GLUTEN-FREE | ONE-PAN

Hearty braised sausage and cabbage make for a traditional German meal. If you prefer, substitute smoked sausage for this recipe's bratwurst.

SERVES 4

Prep Time: 10 minutes

Cook Time: 30 minutes

2 bacon slices, chopped

1 small onion, chopped

3 garlic cloves, minced

1½ pounds green cabbage, cored and sliced

1 cup low-sodium chicken broth

1 tablespoon Dijon mustard

1½ teaspoons caraway seeds

½ teaspoon kosher salt

1¼ pounds bratwurst sausage links

1. Select Convection Roast and preheat the oven to 375°F.

2. In a large cast-iron or other oven-safe skillet, cook the bacon over medium heat until it starts to get crisp and has rendered most of its fat. Add the onion and garlic and cook, stirring, until the vegetables have softened. Add the cabbage and stir to coat with the fat. Pour in the chicken broth and add the mustard, caraway seeds, and salt. Bring to a simmer.

3. Place the sausages on top of the cabbage and transfer the skillet to the oven.

4. Roast for 15 minutes, turn the sausages over, and continue roasting for another 15 minutes, or until the cabbage is soft and the sausages are browned and register 180°F in the center.

SIMPLE SWAP: If you want to use red cabbage instead of green, add 1 tablespoon each of vinegar and brown sugar to the pan. Without acid, red cabbage turns an unappealing shade of blue. The brown sugar cuts the acidity.

SWEET AND SOUR PORK "STIR-FRY"

DAIRY-FREE | GLUTEN-FREE | **ONE-PAN** | UNDER 30 MINUTES

Like the Chinese-Style Pepper Steak "Stir-Fry" (page 86), this stir-fry is really a braise. Pork and vegetables cook in a flavorful liquid, which reduces in the oven to a luscious sauce. Serve the pork as is or over white or brown rice.

SERVES 4

Prep Time: 10 minutes

Cook Time: 15 minutes

1 (1- to 1¼-pound) pork
   tenderloin, cut into
   1-inch pieces

1 teaspoon kosher salt

⅓ cup low-sodium
   chicken broth

2 tablespoons tamari or other
   gluten-free soy sauce

2 tablespoons ketchup
   (gluten-free, if desired)

2 tablespoons brown sugar

2 tablespoons rice vinegar

1 tablespoon toasted
   sesame oil

1 teaspoon cornstarch

1 teaspoon grated ginger

1 red bell pepper, cut into
   1-inch pieces

1 green bell pepper, cut into
   1-inch pieces

6 scallions, white parts cut into
   ½-inch pieces, and green
   parts thinly sliced

1 cup fresh or canned
   pineapple chunks, drained

1. Select Convection Roast and preheat the oven to 375°F.

2. Sprinkle the pork with the salt and set aside.

3. In a 9-by-13-inch baking pan, combine the chicken broth, tamari, ketchup, brown sugar, vinegar, oil, cornstarch, and ginger. Stir to combine.

4. Add the bell peppers and scallion whites and toss to coat with the sauce.

5. Roast the vegetables for 6 minutes. Add the pork and pineapple and gently stir to combine.

6. Roast for 10 minutes, or until the vegetables are tender and the pork is cooked through. Serve, garnished with the scallion greens.

SIMPLE SWAP: Sub in chunks of boneless, skinless chicken breast for the pork.

JERK PORK AND SWEET POTATOES

DAIRY-FREE | GLUTEN-FREE

Jerk pork is usually made with a whole pork shoulder, slow-cooked in a pit or over a low fire on a grill. It takes a really long time and makes a lot of pork. This recipe uses country-style strips of pork shoulder, either with or without bones. Make sure that your ribs are cut from the shoulder and not the loin, which is too lean for this recipe.

SERVES 4

Prep Time: 10 minutes, plus
  20 minutes to marinate
Cook Time: 1½ hours

¼ cup tamari or other gluten-free soy sauce

1 habanero chile, quartered and seeded

3 or 4 scallions, cut into chunks

2 garlic cloves, lightly smashed

2 tablespoons brown sugar

2 tablespoons sherry vinegar

1 tablespoon grated ginger

3 teaspoons ground allspice, divided

1½ teaspoons kosher salt, divided

1 teaspoon dried thyme

2½ pounds bone-in country-style pork shoulder ribs

2 large sweet potatoes, peeled and cut into 1-inch chunks

2 tablespoons olive oil

1. In a blender or food processor, purée the tamari, habanero, scallions, garlic, brown sugar, vinegar, ginger, 2 teaspoons of allspice, ½ teaspoon of salt, and the thyme. Put the ribs in a zip-top bag and pour in the marinade. Seal the bag, pushing out as much air as possible. Refrigerate for at least 20 minutes or overnight.

2. Select Convection Roast and preheat the oven to 225°F.

3. Remove the ribs from the marinade, reserving the marinade, and place them on a sheet pan. Roast for 40 minutes.

4. Baste the ribs with the reserved marinade and roast for another 30 minutes.

5. Meanwhile, in a large bowl, toss the sweet potato chunks with the oil, remaining 1 teaspoon of allspice, and remaining 1 teaspoon of salt.

6. Increase the oven temperature to 325°F. Add the sweet potatoes to the pan with the ribs and roast for 20 to 25 minutes, until the ribs are browned and the sweet potatoes are tender.

SAVE FOR LATER: This marinade will keep for up to a week in the refrigerator, so feel free to double the recipe, and use it on chicken wings or thighs for easy weeknight meals.

SHAWARMA-STYLE LAMB LOIN CHOPS AND POTATOES

GLUTEN-FREE

These spicy yogurt-marinated lamb loin chops are reminiscent of shawarma, the Middle Eastern dish of meat cooked on a spit. The potatoes make a tasty side. Round out the meal with the Roasted Carrots with Cumin-Orange Vinaigrette (page 33).

SERVES 4

Prep Time: 10 minutes

Cook Time: 25 minutes

Nonstick cooking spray

8 (½-inch-thick) lamb loin chops (about 2 pounds)

2 teaspoons kosher salt, divided

⅓ cup plain whole-milk yogurt

2 tablespoons freshly squeezed lemon juice

3 garlic cloves, minced or lightly smashed

1 teaspoon ground cumin

1 teaspoon smoked paprika

¼ teaspoon ground allspice

¼ teaspoon freshly ground black pepper

¼ teaspoon red pepper flakes

12 ounces small red potatoes, quartered

1 tablespoon olive oil

1. Position the top oven rack about 8 inches from the broiling element. Select Convection Roast and preheat the oven to 375°F. Spray a sheet pan with cooking spray.

2. Season the lamb chops on both sides with 1 teaspoon of salt and let sit while you prepare the marinade.

3. In a large bowl, whisk together the yogurt, lemon juice, garlic, cumin, paprika, remaining 1 teaspoon of salt, the allspice, pepper, and red pepper flakes. Pour the marinade into a zip-top bag, leaving 2 tablespoons of marinade in the bowl. Put the lamb chops in the bag. Squeeze out as much air as possible and massage the bag to coat the chops with the marinade. Set aside.

4. Add the potatoes and oil to the bowl with the remaining marinade and toss to coat. Transfer the potatoes to the prepared sheet pan and roast for 15 minutes.

5. Remove the pan from the oven and turn the oven to Convection Broil. Select the High setting if possible. Remove the chops from the marinade, draining off all but a thin coating. Place the chops on the pan with the potatoes (discard the excess marinade).

6. Broil the chops and potatoes for 5 minutes. Flip the chops and stir the potatoes. Broil for another 5 to 6 minutes, until the lamb's internal temperature reads 145°F (for medium-rare). Continue broiling for a few minutes more if you want the meat more done. Let the chops rest for a few minutes, then serve with the potatoes.

EVEN EASIER: Instead of the yogurt marinade, brush the chops and toss the potatoes with vegetable oil, and sprinkle with a hot Madras curry powder (I like the one from Penzeys).

LAMB CURRY

GLUTEN-FREE

You can adjust this warm-spiced lamb curry's heat level: If you prefer a mild heat level, omit the crushed red pepper. Serve the stew over steamed rice or couscous.

SERVES 4

*Prep Time: 10 minutes, plus
  2 hours to marinate*

Cook Time: 1½ hours

2 small onions

2 garlic cloves, lightly smashed

1¼ cups plain whole-milk yogurt

1 tablespoon cornstarch

1 tablespoon ground coriander

2 teaspoons ground cumin

2 teaspoons kosher salt

1½ teaspoons freshly ground
   black pepper

1 teaspoon ground allspice

½ teaspoon ground
   dried ginger

½ teaspoon red pepper
   flakes (optional)

1½ pounds boneless
   lamb shoulder, cut into
   1½-inch pieces

¼ cup chopped fresh mint

1. Cut one of the onions into chunks. In a blender or food processor, combine the onion, garlic, yogurt, cornstarch, coriander, cumin, salt, black pepper, allspice, ginger, and red pepper flakes (if using). Blend until mostly smooth.

2. Put the lamb in a large bowl and pour the yogurt mixture over it. Stir to coat the meat evenly, then cover and let marinate at room temperature for 2 hours or in the refrigerator overnight.

3. Select Convection Roast and preheat the oven to 350°F.

4. Pour the meat and marinade into a large Dutch oven. Slice the second onion and add it to the pot. Cover the pot and bake for about 1½ hours, until the lamb is very tender. Serve garnished with the fresh mint.

SIMPLE SWAP: If you aren't a fan of lamb or can't find lamb shoulder, you can substitute beef chuck roast.

SOFT PRETZELS page 110

BREADS AND SAVORY PASTRIES

CHEDDAR-SESAME CRACKERS

VEGETARIAN

If you're a fan of commercial cheese crackers, you owe it to yourself to try these crackers. The dough is similar to that of cheese straws, but it's rolled thin to produce a fabulous crunchy texture. If you want to get fancy, you can use small cookie cutters to make decorative shapes, rerolling the dough and chilling as necessary.

MAKES ABOUT 36

Prep Time: 15 minutes, plus 20 minutes to chill

Cook Time: 20 minutes

1¼ cups all-purpose flour

¼ teaspoon kosher salt

¼ teaspoon cayenne

10 tablespoons (1¼ stick) cold unsalted butter, cut into small pieces

4 ounces sharp Cheddar cheese, shredded

½ cup toasted sesame seeds

1. In a food processor, combine the flour, salt, and cayenne and pulse to combine. Add the butter pieces and pulse until the dough forms clumps, stopping occasionally to scrape down the sides of the bowl. Add the cheese and sesame seeds and pulse to combine. Turn the dough out onto a lightly floured board and knead it briefly to bring it together.

2. Roll out the dough between two sheets of parchment paper to a ¼-inch thickness. Chill until firm, about 20 minutes.

3. Select Convection Bake and preheat the oven to 350°F. Line two sheet pans with silicone baking mats (or use one sheet pan and bake in batches).

4. Remove the top sheet of parchment. Using a bench scraper or sharp knife, cut the dough into 1-by-2-inch rectangles. Transfer the crackers to the prepared sheet pans, leaving a ½-inch space around the crackers.

5. Bake for 16 to 20 minutes, until the crackers are set and golden brown. Let cool on the pans for at least 10 minutes, then transfer to a rack to cool completely.

FOR COUNTERTOP OVENS: You will have to bake the crackers in batches, but the dough will keep in the refrigerator for up to 2 days or in the freezer for up to 1 month, so feel free to make smaller batches.

SOFT PRETZELS

VEGETARIAN

Soft pretzels aren't as hard to make as you might imagine. The secret? Boiling the pretzels in water mixed with baking soda before baking gives them a shiny, chewy exterior. Try serving them with mustard.

MAKES 8 PRETZELS

Prep Time: 20 minutes, plus
40 minutes to rise

Cook Time: 15 minutes

½ cup warm water plus
  2 quarts water, for boiling

2 tablespoons sugar

1½ teaspoons kosher salt, plus
  more for sprinkling

1 (¼-ounce) packet active
  dry yeast

4 cups all-purpose flour

Nonstick cooking spray

½ cup baking soda

1 large egg, beaten

1. In a large bowl, combine ½ cup of warm water, sugar, and kosher salt. Stir in the yeast and let the mixture rest until it starts to foam. Stir in the flour, then transfer the dough to a floured board and knead for 6 to 8 minutes, until the dough is smooth. Wipe out the bowl and spray with cooking spray. Return the dough to the bowl and cover with plastic wrap or a clean towel. Let rest in a warm place for 35 to 40 minutes, until the dough has risen by about half.

2. Select Convection Bake and preheat the oven to 425°F. Line two sheet pans with silicone baking mats (or use one sheet pan and bake in batches).

3. In a large pot, bring the 2 quarts of water and baking soda to a boil.

4. Meanwhile, punch the dough down and divide it into 8 pieces. Roll out each piece into a 24-inch rope. One at a time, shape the pretzels. Bring the ends toward yourself into an upside-down horseshoe. Cross one side over the other, then cross the second side back over the first to form a traditional pretzel twist. Press the ends against the dough to seal. Place on the prepared sheet pan and repeat with the remaining ropes.

5. Gently lower the pretzels into the boiling water, one or two at a time, and boil for 20 to 30 seconds. Using a large slotted spatula, remove them from the water and place them back on the pan.

6. Brush the tops of the pretzels with the beaten egg and sprinkle with additional kosher salt. Bake for 12 to 14 minutes, until dark golden brown. Let cool for a minute, then transfer to a rack for 5 to 10 minutes.

FOR COUNTERTOP OVENS: You'll need to bake the pretzels in smaller batches. Start the first batch baking while you boil the second batch to save time.

CAJUN CORNBREAD

VEGETARIAN

Plain cornbread is delicious. Even the boxed mixes aren't half bad. But this recipe takes cornbread to spicy and cheesy heights. A convection oven produces a beautifully browned top with a soft, crumbly interior.

SERVES 6 TO 8

Prep Time: 10 minutes

Cook Time: 25 minutes

2 tablespoons vegetable oil, divided

¼ cup chopped onion

¼ cup chopped red bell pepper

1 cup all-purpose flour

1 cup cornmeal

¼ cup grated Parmesan cheese

1 tablespoon sugar

1 tablespoon baking powder

2 teaspoons Cajun or Creole seasoning

½ teaspoon kosher salt

1 cup whole milk

4 tablespoons (½ stick) unsalted butter, melted and slightly cooled

2 large eggs

1. Select Convection Bake and preheat the oven to 375°F. Pour 1 tablespoon of oil in a 10-inch cast-iron skillet and place the skillet in the oven to heat.

2. In a small skillet, heat the remaining 1 tablespoon of oil over medium-high heat. Add the onion and bell pepper and cook, stirring occasionally, for about 5 minutes, or until soft. Set aside to cool.

3. In a large bowl, whisk together the flour, cornmeal, Parmesan, sugar, baking powder, Cajun seasoning, and salt.

4. In a small bowl, whisk together the milk, melted butter, and eggs. Pour the milk mixture into the flour mixture and stir to combine. Gently stir in the onion and bell pepper.

5. Remove the skillet from the oven and pour in the batter, smoothing out the top. Bake for 25 to 30 minutes, until the top is golden brown and the edges are pulling away from the pan.

6. Let cool for 5 minutes, then run a knife around the sides and turn the cornbread out onto a rack to cool for another 10 minutes.

HELPFUL HACK: Using a hot cast-iron skillet produces a browned, crunchy crust on the bottom and sides of the cornbread. If you prefer softer crusts, use a 9-inch square baking pan sprayed with cooking spray or coated with butter, and don't preheat the pan before baking the cornbread.

BUTTERY PAN ROLLS

VEGETARIAN

These rolls are easy to make because the yeast dough requires no kneading and no rolling or shaping.

MAKES 15 ROLLS

Prep Time: 10 minutes, plus 1 hour 15 minutes to rise

Cook Time: 15 minutes

2 (¼-ounce) packets active dry yeast

½ cup warm water

4½ cups all-purpose flour

2 tablespoons sugar

1½ teaspoons kosher salt

1 large egg, beaten

1 cup warm milk

¾ cup (1½ sticks) unsalted butter, melted, divided

1. In a large bowl, dissolve the yeast in the warm water and let stand until bubbly, about 15 minutes.

2. Add about half the flour, the sugar, and salt and stir until well combined. Add the egg, warm milk, and 6 tablespoons of melted butter. Beat for a few minutes until thoroughly combined. Stir in the remaining flour.

3. Cover the bowl with plastic wrap or a clean towel, and let rise in a warm place until doubled in volume, about 45 minutes.

4. Pour 3 tablespoons of the remaining melted butter in a 9-by-13-inch baking pan and tilt the pan to spread it evenly. Briefly beat down the batter and spoon it out into 15 fairly even scoops in the pan. Cover lightly and let rise until almost doubled, about 30 minutes.

5. Select Convection Bake and preheat the oven to 400°F.

6. Drizzle the remaining 3 tablespoons of melted butter over the rolls. Bake for 13 to 15 minutes, until golden brown and puffed. Let cool for a few minutes and serve warm.

SIMPLE SWAP: After drizzling the melted butter on the tops of the rolls, sprinkle them with sesame seeds, poppy seeds, or Parmesan cheese, then bake as directed.

CHIVE AND PARMESAN POPOVERS

VEGETARIAN

Like a Dutch Baby (page 19), a popover is airy and eggy. This recipe elevates the traditional popover with the addition of cheese and herbs.

SERVES 6

Prep Time: 10 minutes

Cook Time: 35 minutes

4 tablespoons
 (½ stick) unsalted butter,
 melted, divided

2 cups whole milk

4 large eggs

2 cups all-purpose flour

1 teaspoon kosher salt

½ teaspoon freshly ground
 black pepper

3 tablespoons chopped
 fresh chives

½ cup grated Parmesan
 cheese, divided

1. Select Convection Bake and preheat the oven to 425°F.

2. With a pastry brush, liberally coat the bottoms and sides of a 12-cup popover or muffin tin with 3 tablespoons of melted butter. Place the pan in the oven while it heats.

3. In a large bowl, whisk together the milk, eggs, and remaining 1 tablespoon of butter until well blended. Add the flour, salt, pepper, chives, and ¼ cup of Parmesan. Mix well.

4. Carefully remove the hot pan from the oven and use a small ladle or liquid measuring cup to fill the cups evenly with the batter. Gently sprinkle the remaining ¼ cup of cheese evenly over the cups.

5. Bake for 20 minutes, then reduce the oven temperature to 375°F, but don't open the oven. Continue baking until the popovers are deep golden brown, 15 to 18 more minutes. Cool briefly in the pan and serve warm.

FOR COUNTERTOP OVENS: You'll need to use a 6-cup popover or muffin tin. You can either bake two batches or halve the recipe.

SIMPLE SWAP: Use whatever herbs and cheese you like. Oregano and Gruyère is another one of my favorite combinations.

"EVERYTHING" BISCUIT ROLLS

VEGETARIAN | UNDER 30 MINUTES

The idea for these rolls came from my trusty Sunset *bread book. The original version was a very rich biscuit dough rolled around in toasted sesame seeds and cut into pinwheel rolls. Here they are with the seasoning mix from "everything" bagels. This super simple dough is inspired by a shortcut made popular by cookbook authors Nathalie Dupree and Kenji López-Alt, among others. I add a little sour cream to their basic mix of equal parts self-rising flour and heavy cream.*

MAKES 12 BISCUITS

Prep Time: 10 minutes

Cook Time: 15 minutes

2 tablespoons toasted sesame seeds

2 tablespoons poppy seeds

2 tablespoons dried minced onion

2 tablespoons dried minced garlic

2 teaspoons kosher salt

2 cups self-rising flour

¼ cup sour cream

1 cup heavy cream

2 to 3 tablespoons all-purpose flour, for dusting

1 large egg, beaten, divided

1. Select Convection Bake and preheat the oven to 425°F.

2. In a small bowl, stir together the sesame seeds, poppy seeds, onion, garlic, and salt. Set aside.

3. In a large bowl, stir together the self-rising flour, sour cream, and cream until combined. Scoop out the dough onto a lightly floured board.

4. Knead briefly until it holds its shape. Press out into a 6-by-8-inch rectangle. Fold the dough over in thirds, then press out into a rectangle again and repeat folding once more.

5. Roll out the dough into a 10-by-12-inch rectangle. Brush with half the beaten egg, then sprinkle the spice mixture over evenly.

6. Starting at a long side, roll the dough up into a cylinder and pinch the seam down to adhere to the dough. Use a bench scraper or a sharp knife to cut the roll into 1-inch pieces.

7. Line a large sheet pan with a silicone mat and place the rolls, cut-side up, on the pan, spaced evenly. Brush the rolls with the remaining egg.

8. Bake for 12 to 15 minutes, or until deep golden brown. Let cool for 5 to 10 minutes before serving.

FOR COUNTERTOP OVENS: You can fit all the rolls onto a 9-by-13-inch sheet pan. They will rise enough to touch while baking, which will help them rise, but they won't be browned on the sides. If you prefer completely browned rolls, bake the rolls in two batches.

EVEN EASIER: "Everything" spice mix is available online and in many grocery stores.

MULTIGRAIN SANDWICH BREAD

VEGETARIAN

For a whole-grain bread, this bread is surprisingly light in texture, but it's still sturdy enough to make a great sandwich bread. To ensure the correct density, don't let it rise longer than 20 minutes during the second rise.

MAKES 1 LOAF

Prep Time: 10 minutes, plus
1 hour to rise

Cook Time: 55 minutes

¾ cup rolled oats

2 tablespoons finely ground bulgur wheat

2 tablespoons unsalted butter

3 tablespoons brown sugar

2 teaspoons kosher salt

1 cup boiling water

2 (¼-ounce) packets active dry yeast

¾ cup warm milk

¼ cup toasted sesame seeds

2 cups all-purpose flour

1 cup whole-wheat flour

1. In a large bowl, combine the oatmeal, bulgur wheat, butter, brown sugar, and salt. Pour the boiling water over the mixture and stir to combine. Let cool to room temperature, stirring occasionally.

2. In a small bowl, dissolve the yeast in the warm milk. After a few minutes, when it's starting to bubble, pour it into the grain mixture. Add the sesame seeds and both flours and stir to combine.

3. Knead the dough on a floured board for about 10 minutes. The dough will be soft but should not be sticky.

4. Place in an oiled bowl and cover the bowl with plastic wrap or a clean towel. Let rise in a warm place until doubled in size, about 40 minutes.

5. Oil a 9-by-5-inch loaf pan. Punch the dough down and pat out into an 8-by-10-inch rectangle. Starting with a short side, pull the sides into the center to form a loaf shape. Place the dough in the prepared pan, seam-side down. Cover with plastic wrap and let rise for 20 minutes, but no longer.

6. Select Convection Bake and preheat the oven to 350°F.

7. Bake the loaf for 50 to 55 minutes, until the top is browned and the bread sounds hollow when tapped. Let cool for 5 minutes, then remove from the pan and cool completely on a rack.

FOR COUNTERTOP OVENS: Place the oven rack in its lowest position so the bread has room to rise.

ONION-DILL BRAID

VEGETARIAN

This bread uses both fresh dill and dill seed. It goes great with soup or salad for a light meal.

MAKES 1 LOAF

Prep Time: 20 minutes, plus
2 hours to rise

Cook Time: 35 minutes

1 (¼-ounce) packet active
    dry yeast

¼ cup warm water

3 cups all-purpose flour

1 cup sour cream

1 large egg

¼ cup finely chopped onion

¼ cup chopped fresh dill

2 tablespoons sugar

1 tablespoon unsalted
    butter, melted

1 tablespoon dill seed

2 teaspoons kosher salt

Nonstick cooking spray

1 tablespoon heavy
    (whipping) cream

1. In a large bowl, dissolve the yeast in the warm water and let sit for 5 minutes, or until bubbling.

2. Stir in 1 cup of flour, the sour cream, egg, onion, fresh dill, sugar, melted butter, dill seed, and salt. Beat by hand until well blended.

3. Stir in as much of the remaining flour as possible, then turn the dough out onto a floured board and knead in the rest until the dough is soft but not sticky. Form it into a ball.

4. Clean the bowl, then spray it with cooking spray. Place the dough in the bowl, turning to coat with the oil. Cover with plastic wrap or a clean towel, and let rise in a warm place until doubled in size, 60 to 75 minutes.

5. Punch the dough down and divide it into three equal pieces. Cover the pieces and let rest for 10 to 15 minutes. Roll each piece into a 16- to 18-inch rope.

6. Spray a sheet pan with cooking spray. Place the three ropes side by side on the pan. Pinch the top ends of the ropes together and braid them, then pinch the bottom ends together. Cover lightly with plastic wrap or a clean towel and let rise for 30 minutes, until almost doubled.

7. Select Convection Bake and preheat the oven to 350°F.

8. Brush the braid with the cream and bake for 35 to 40 minutes, until the top is golden brown and the bread sounds hollow when tapped. Let cool before slicing.

EVEN EASIER: Although the braided bread is aesthetically striking, you can skip that step and just bake the ball of dough in a loaf pan.

OLIVE FOCACCIA

DAIRY-FREE | VEGAN | ONE-PAN

Focaccia is an Italian flatbread flavored with olive oil and often topped with cheese or herbs and olives. Unlike other flatbreads, focaccia is light and soft. It makes a delightful accompaniment to an antipasto platter or salad.

SERVES 6 TO 8

Prep Time: 20 minutes, plus 2 hours 10 minutes to rise

Cook Time: 20 minutes

2 teaspoons sugar

2 cups warm water

1 (¼-ounce) packet active dry yeast

4½ cups all-purpose flour, plus more for kneading

2 teaspoons kosher salt

4 tablespoons extra-virgin olive oil, divided, plus more for dipping (optional)

1 cup black or green pitted olives (such as kalamata or Greek), very coarsely chopped

1 tablespoon fresh thyme leaves

1. In a large bowl, stir the sugar into the warm water. Sprinkle in the yeast, and stir with a fork. Let stand until the yeast dissolves, about 10 minutes.

2. Add the flour, salt, and 1 tablespoon of oil and stir to blend well (the dough will be sticky). Knead the dough on a floured surface, adding more flour as necessary, until smooth and elastic, about 10 minutes. Form the dough into a ball. Oil a large bowl and add the dough, turning to coat. Cover the bowl with plastic wrap or a warm towel and let rise in a warm area until doubled, about 1 hour.

3. Punch down the dough; knead into a ball again, and return to the same bowl. Cover with plastic wrap and let rise until doubled, about 45 minutes.

4. Coat a sheet pan with 1 tablespoon of the oil. Punch down the dough and transfer it to the pan. Press the dough out into a rectangle that fills the pan. Using your fingertips, make even indentations all over the dough. Drizzle the remaining 2 tablespoons of oil over the dough. Sprinkle evenly with the olives and thyme. Let the dough rise, uncovered, until puffy, about 25 minutes.

5. Select Convection Bake and preheat the oven to 475°F. Bake the focaccia until brown and crusty, about 20 minutes. Serve warm or at room temperature, with additional oil for dipping, if desired.

SIMPLE SWAP: Focaccia is great with all kinds of toppings (or plain, for that matter). Try replacing the olives with roasted marinated peppers from the Roasted Tri-Color Pepper Salad (page 28) or chopped Roasted Mushrooms (page 30).

CHORIZO-POTATO EMPANADAS

This recipe uses the taco's popular combo of potatoes and chorizo as a filling for empanadas. Instead of fried potatoes, it calls for potato flakes to thicken the chorizo liquid. Try serving the empanadas with salsa or guacamole on the side.

SERVES 4 AS A MAIN COURSE; 6 TO 8 AS AN APPETIZER

Prep Time: 30 minutes

Cook Time: 20 minutes

---

1 pound fresh Mexican chorizo

1 small onion, chopped

⅔ cup water

⅔ cup mashed potato flakes

4 ounces cream cheese

1 (14-ounce) package refrigerated pie dough (2 crusts)

1 large egg, beaten

1. Select Convection Roast and preheat the oven to 375°F.

2. In a large skillet, cook the chorizo over medium heat, breaking it up as it browns. When it is almost done, 5 or 6 minutes, add the onion and stir to combine, cooking until the onion is softened. Add the water and heat to a simmer.

3. Stir the potato flakes into the liquid. Add the cream cheese and stir until the potatoes are rehydrated and the cream cheese is melted.

4. Unroll one piecrust on a cutting board. Pinch together any tears. Using a 4-inch round pastry cutter or a parchment circle as a guide, cut out circles; you should get 5 circles from one crust. Repeat with the other piecrust. Combine the scraps into a ball and roll out into an oval the same thickness as the original crust. Cut out additional rounds (you'll probably get another 3 or 4).

5. Spoon 2 tablespoons of filling on half of one dough circle, spreading it out to about ½ inch from the edges. Fold the other side over the filling and seal the edges, brushing a little of the beaten egg along the edge if needed. Press the tines of a fork around the edge to crimp. Repeat with the other dough circles and remaining filling.

6. Place all the empanadas on a sheet pan. Cut two small slits in the top of each empanada and brush with the egg.

7. Bake for 18 to 20 minutes, until golden brown. Let cool for a few minutes before serving.

SIMPLE SWAP: If you can't find Mexican chorizo, substitute 1 pound of ground pork seasoned with 3 tablespoons of Mexican seasoning.

THIN-CRUST PIZZA

ONE-PAN | UNDER 30 MINUTES

The even heat and relatively high effective temperature of the convection oven allows pizza to set before it rises, leaving it crisp instead of doughy. Try topping this pizza with sliced Roasted Mushrooms (page 30), 8 ounces thinly sliced pepperoni, or 8 ounces cooked Italian sausage—add them on top of the first layer of mozzarella cheese.

SERVES 4

Prep Time: 15 minutes

Cook Time: 10 minutes

1 pound refrigerated
   pizza dough

3 tablespoons extra-virgin olive
   oil, divided

½ cup marinara sauce or
   pizza sauce

6 ounces shredded
   mozzarella cheese

½ cup coarsely shredded
   Parmesan cheese

1. Select Convection Roast and preheat oven to 450°F. Place a sheet pan in the oven as it heats.

2. Punch down the pizza dough to release as much air as possible. Tear off two large pieces of parchment paper. Coat the dough with 1 tablespoon of oil and place it between the sheets. Press out the dough to a size that fits the sheet pan.

3. Remove the sheet pan from the oven and brush it with 1 tablespoon of the remaining oil. Peel off the top piece of parchment paper from the dough and flip it over onto the sheet pan. Remove the second piece of parchment.

4. Spread the marinara sauce over the dough. You should be able to see the dough through the sauce in places; you don't want a thick coating. Evenly top the sauce with about half the mozzarella cheese.

5. Bake for 6 minutes.

6. Remove the pan from the oven and sprinkle the remaining mozzarella and the Parmesan cheese over the pizza. Continue baking for another 3 to 5 minutes, until the top is bubbling and the crust is deep golden brown.

7. Transfer the pizza to a wire rack to cool for a few minutes, then transfer to a cutting board to slice and serve.

FOR COUNTERTOP OVENS: You'll need to make two half-size pizzas using a smaller pan, and bake them separately. Slide the second pizza into the oven as you're cooling the first one, and by the time you're done eating the first one, the second one will be ready.

HELPFUL HACK: For an extra-crisp browned crust, use a pizza peel, cake lifter, or even a very large spatula to slide the pizza off the pan after you have added the second layer of cheese, and cook it directly on the oven rack for the remaining time.

CHERRY AND PEAR GALETTE page 136

DESSERTS AND SWEETS

OVEN CARAMEL CORN

GLUTEN-FREE | VEGETARIAN

It might seem odd to make this delicious snack in the oven, but the even heat and fan of a convection oven turns out perfectly crunchy, buttery caramel corn every time. You can pop the corn however you'd like; you'll need to start with about ¾ cup of kernels. If you use microwave popcorn, go with a "natural" version, such as Paul Newman or Orville Redenbacher.

SERVES 4

Prep Time: 10 minutes

Cook Time: 1 hour

Nonstick cooking spray

24 cups popped popcorn, lightly salted

1 cup (2 sticks) unsalted butter

2 cups light brown sugar (packed)

½ cup dark corn syrup

1 teaspoon baking soda

1. Select Convection Bake and preheat the oven to 250°F.

2. Spray a large roasting pan with cooking spray. Put the popcorn in the pan.

3. In a large saucepan, melt the butter over medium-high heat. Add the brown sugar and corn syrup and stir to combine. Bring to a vigorous boil, then reduce the heat to medium-low and let simmer undisturbed for 5 minutes. Turn off the heat and slowly whisk in the baking soda. The mixture will bubble up and turn lighter in color. Immediately pour the caramel over the popcorn, being sure to scrape the caramel off the bottom of the pot. Toss until the popcorn is coated with the caramel. Don't worry if it's not evenly distributed over the popcorn; it will even out as it bakes.

4. Bake for 1 hour, stirring every 15 minutes, until the caramel corn has turned a deep amber color. Transfer the caramel corn to a sheet pan lined with a silicone baking mat or parchment paper to cool. Once the caramel corn reaches room temperature, use your hands or a spoon to break it up, then store it in an airtight container for up to 1 week.

FOR COUNTERTOP OVENS: Since you won't be able to fit a roasting pan in a smaller oven, make half a batch and bake in a deep 9-by-13-inch pan.

SIMPLE SWAP: If you like, substitute a can of salted roasted peanuts or almonds for about 2 cups of the popcorn.

MEXICAN BROWNIES

VEGETARIAN

These fudgy brownies are not terribly sweet. For a sweeter brownie, use a chocolate in the range of 55 percent cocoa, and for a firmer but chewy brownie, increase the baking time by 5 minutes. Try topping these brownies with coffee ice cream and dulce de leche.

SERVES 8

Prep Time: 10 minutes

Cook Time: 25 minutes

½ cup (1 stick) unsalted butter, plus more for greasing

8 ounces dark chocolate (60 to 72 percent cocoa)

1 cup sugar

2 teaspoons vanilla extract

Pinch salt

2 large eggs, at room temperature

1 teaspoon ground cinnamon

¼ teaspoon cayenne

¾ cup all-purpose flour

1. Select Convection Bake and preheat the oven to 350°F.

2. Line a 9-inch square baking pan with aluminum foil, with the ends extending over the edges of the pan on two sides. Butter the foil and pan.

3. In a small saucepan, gently melt the butter and chocolate together over low heat, stirring, just until melted. Remove from the heat and let cool slightly. Pour into a large bowl.

4. Stir in the sugar, vanilla, and salt. Add the eggs, one at a time, and stir until completely blended.

5. Mix the cinnamon and cayenne into the flour until evenly dispersed. Add the flour to the chocolate mixture and beat until incorporated, about a minute. The batter may be a bit grainy looking.

6. Pour the batter into the prepared pan and bake for 25 to 30 minutes, until a toothpick inserted into the center comes out with crumbs but no raw batter sticking to it. Let cool for about 10 minutes. Pick up the edges of the foil and carefully lift the brownies out of the pan. Peel off the foil and let cool for another 5 minutes. Cut into squares.

SIMPLE SWAP: If you prefer plain chocolate brownies, just leave out the cinnamon and cayenne. In this case, the brownies are wonderful with vanilla ice cream and raspberry sauce.

SAVE FOR LATER: This recipe is dead-easy to scale up, so if you have two baking pans, you can double the recipe and freeze the extra brownies. Wrapped airtight, they'll keep for a month.

GINGERBREAD CAKE TWO WAYS

DAIRY-FREE OPTION | VEGETARIAN

This recipe's oil and hot water batter produces a dense cake that stays moist for days. Try serving it with a brandy glaze or with whipped cream mixed with lemon curd. Both options are described here.

SERVES 6 TO 8

Prep Time: 15 minutes

Cook Time: 30 minutes

FOR THE CAKE

½ cup very hot water

½ cup vegetable oil

½ cup packed brown sugar

½ cup molasses

1 large egg

1½ cups all-purpose flour

1½ teaspoons ground ginger

¾ teaspoon ground cinnamon

½ teaspoon kosher salt

½ teaspoon baking powder

½ teaspoon baking soda

1. **To make the cake:** Select Convection Bake and preheat the oven to 350°F. Grease and flour a 9-inch square baking pan.

2. In a large bowl, combine the water and oil.

3. Add the sugar, molasses, and egg and beat until smooth.

4. In a medium bowl, whisk together the flour, ginger, cinnamon, salt, baking powder, and baking soda. Add the dry ingredients to the wet mixture and beat well.

5. Pour the batter into the prepared pan and bake for about 30 minutes (check it at 25 minutes; the cake is done when a toothpick inserted in the center comes out clean).

6. If you're going to make the brandy glaze, use a bamboo or metal skewer to poke the gingerbread all over at 1-inch intervals while it's still warm.

FOR THE LEMON CREAM

1 cup heavy (whipping) cream

1 cup lemon curd

FOR THE BRANDY GLAZE

5 cardamom pods

2 tablespoons brandy

2 tablespoons water

¼ cup packed brown sugar

1 tablespoon freshly squeezed
lemon juice

EVEN EASIER: Skip the lemon cream or the brandy glaze and top the cake with plain whipped cream.

7. **To make the lemon cream:** Pour the cream into a chilled bowl and whip with a hand mixer on medium to high speed until thickened; the cream should hold soft peaks but not look clumpy or grainy. If you get to that stage, simply add a little more liquid cream and mix on low speed until it smooths out.

8. Fold a quarter of the whipped cream into the lemon curd: Gently scoop the cream and let it fall back into the curd, rotate the bowl a quarter turn, and repeat. Continue until the two are mixed evenly.

9. Fold the rest of the plain whipped cream into the curd base using the same method. Chill if not using immediately.

10. To serve, slice the cake and top with a spoonful of lemon cream.

11. **To make the brandy glaze:** In a small saucepan, simmer the cardamom pods in the brandy and water until the liquid is reduced by half.

12. Add the brown sugar and lemon juice. Bring to a boil and cook just until the sugar is dissolved. Let cool for several minutes, then pour over the gingerbread. Let rest for 20 minutes to let the syrup soak in, then slice and serve.

CHERRY AND PEAR GALETTE

DAIRY-FREE | VEGETARIAN | ONE-PAN

A galette differs from a traditional pie or tart in that it's formed and baked freeform, without a tart pan or pie plate. This recipe calls for a store-bought piecrust.

SERVES 6

Prep Time: 15 minutes

Cook Time: 20 minutes

2 large pears, peeled and cut into ½-inch chunks (about 2 cups)

2 cups frozen sweet cherries, thawed and drained

⅓ cup sugar, plus 2 tablespoons

2 tablespoons all-purpose flour

¼ teaspoon ground cinnamon

½ teaspoon grated lemon zest (optional)

Pinch kosher salt

1 (9-inch) refrigerated piecrust

2 teaspoons unsalted butter, cut into pea-size pieces

1 large egg, beaten

1. Select Convection Bake and preheat the oven to 350°F.

2. In a medium bowl, gently mix the pears and cherries with ⅓ cup of sugar, the flour, cinnamon, lemon zest (if using), and salt.

3. Unroll the piecrust on a sheet pan, patching any tears. Spoon the fruit mixture into the center of the crust, leaving a border of about 1½ inches around the edges. Distribute the butter pieces over the fruit. Fold the outside edge of the crust around the outer edge of the fruit, making pleats as necessary, but leaving most of the fruit exposed. Brush the crust with the egg. Sprinkle the remaining 2 tablespoons of sugar over the crust and fruit.

4. Bake for 12 to 15 minutes. Check the galette and rotate the pan if the crust is not browning evenly. Continue baking until the crust is deep golden brown and the fruit is bubbling, about 5 more minutes.

5. Let cool for 10 minutes, then cut into wedges and serve warm.

SIMPLE SWAP: Galettes are delicious with just about any fruit or combination thereof. Peach and raspberry is another of my favorite combinations.

OATMEAL CRISPIES

DAIRY-FREE | VEGETARIAN

These slice-and-bake cookies are so easy to make. Make the dough and bake just a few at a time for an after-school snack. Or breakfast. (Oatmeal! It's healthy!)

MAKES 5 DOZEN

Prep Time: 10 minutes, plus
*   1 hour to chill*
Cook Time: 25 minutes

1 cup vegetable shortening
1 cup brown sugar
1 cup granulated sugar
2 large eggs
1 teaspoon vanilla extract
1½ cups all-purpose flour
1 teaspoon kosher salt
1 teaspoon baking soda
3 cups quick-cook oatmeal

SAVE FOR LATER: This recipe makes a lot of cookies, but rather than cut it in half, I usually make the whole batch of dough and freeze half. That way, you can cut cookies and bake a few as you need or want them.

1. In a stand mixer or with a hand mixer, beat together the shortening and both sugars until light and fluffy, about 2 minutes. Add the eggs and vanilla and beat for another 30 to 45 seconds.

2. In a medium bowl, whisk together the flour, salt, and baking soda. Add to the butter and sugar mixture and beat just until combined. Stir in the oatmeal (if using a hand mixer, you may need to do this by hand, as the dough will be quite stiff).

3. Divide the dough into two portions. Shape each half into a roll about 2½ inches in diameter and wrap each roll in plastic wrap or wax paper. Chill for 1 hour in the freezer or several hours in the refrigerator.

4. Select Convection Bake and preheat the oven to 350°F.

5. Slice the rolls into ¼-inch-thick cookies and place them on a sheet pan about 1 inch apart. If you have two sheet pans, you can bake them both at once.

6. Bake for 10 to 12 minutes, until golden brown and firm (the cookies will crisp as they cool). Let them cool completely before serving. Repeat to bake the remaining batches.

EASY BLUEBERRY STREUSEL CAKE

VEGETARIAN

This fast and easy recipe cuts the sweetness of cake with the tartness of blueberries.

SERVES 8

Prep Time: 10 minutes

Cook Time: 25 minutes

Nonstick cooking spray

1 package white or yellow cake mix (for a 2-layer cake)

½ cup (1 stick) unsalted butter, melted

2½ cups blueberries

2 tablespoons sugar

2 teaspoons grated lemon zest

1. Select Convection Bake and preheat the oven to 350°F. Spray a 9-inch square baking pan with cooking spray.

2. In a large bowl, stir together the cake mix and butter. It will be rather dry and a bit lumpy.

3. In a medium bowl, mix together the blueberries, sugar, and lemon zest. Use a potato masher or the back of a large fork to lightly smash some of the berries.

4. Transfer about two-thirds of the cake mixture to the prepared pan, pressing it into an even layer with your fingertips. Spread the blueberry mixture over the mix. Top with the remaining cake mixture, crumbling it over evenly.

5. Bake for 20 to 25 minutes, until the fruit is bubbling and the topping is golden brown.

6. Let cool for at least 15 minutes, then slice and serve.

HELPFUL HACK: It's easy to make this recipe into a bar cookie. Just use closer to three-quarters of the cake mixture in the bottom of the pan to get a very sturdy layer. Bake as directed, but chill before cutting into bars.

BROWN SUGAR SHORTBREAD

VEGETARIAN

This recipe substitutes brown sugar for granulated sugar, producing a shortbread with a richer and more complex flavor.

MAKES 36 BARS

Prep Time: 10 minutes

Cook Time: 40 minutes

Nonstick cooking spray

¾ cup brown sugar

1½ cups (3 sticks) unsalted butter, at room temperature

3 cups all-purpose flour

3 tablespoons cornstarch

½ teaspoon kosher salt

1. Select Convection Bake and preheat the oven to 325°F. Spray a 9-by-13-inch pan with cooking spray and line with parchment paper.

2. In a stand mixer (or with a hand mixer), beat the sugar and butter until well blended and fluffy.

3. In a large bowl, whisk together the flour, cornstarch, and salt. Gradually add the dry ingredients to the butter mixture and mix just until combined. (If you're using a hand mixer, you may have to finish mixing by hand; the dough is quite stiff.)

4. Press the dough into the prepared pan until very even and smooth.

5. Bake the shortbread for 35 to 40 minutes, until light golden brown around the edges. After 20 minutes, check the shortbread, rotating the pan if not browning evenly.

6. Remove the shortbread from the oven and let it cool slightly, then slice (these bars are easiest to cut when they're slightly warm). Let cool before serving.

HELPFUL HACK: If you like your shortbread extra crisp, bake for an additional 5 to 6 minutes, then turn off the oven and keep the pan in for another 10 minutes.

BRANDY PECAN TART

VEGETARIAN

This tart was inspired by baker Carolyn Weil, who uses bourbon instead of brandy.

SERVES 8

Prep Time: 15 minutes, plus
*   25 minutes to chill*
Cook Time: 50 minutes

FOR THE CRUST

1½ cups all-purpose flour

2 teaspoons granulated sugar

¼ teaspoon kosher salt

½ cup (1 stick) cold unsalted
   butter, cut into small cubes

3 tablespoons ice cold water

FOR THE FILLING

1 cup pecan pieces

¼ cup brown sugar

½ cup dark corn syrup

3 large eggs

2 tablespoons brandy

1 teaspoon vanilla extract

⅛ teaspoon kosher salt

1. **To make the crust:** Combine the flour, granulated sugar, and salt in a food processor and pulse briefly to mix. Add the butter and pulse until it is cut uniformly into the flour in very small pieces. Add the water all at once and process just until the dough holds together. Transfer the dough to a zip-top bag and knead briefly, just to combine. Press the dough into a round, thick disk. Chill in the refrigerator for 10 minutes.

2. Remove the dough from the refrigerator and place it between two large pieces of parchment paper. Roll out the dough into a circle about 11 inches in diameter. Peel the parchment paper from the dough. Without stretching the dough, fit it into the bottom of a 9-inch tart pan covering the sides. Trim any excess crust and patch any holes or thin spots.

3. Place the pan in the freezer for 15 minutes or so, until the dough is very stiff. Select Convection Bake and preheat the oven to 350°F.

4. Remove the crust from the freezer and line it with a piece of aluminum foil. Pour in pie weights, pennies, dried beans, or rice to weigh it down. For easy moving, place the tart pan on a sheet pan. Bake for 20 minutes. Remove the pan from the oven and carefully lift the foil and pie weights out of the crust. The crust should be set and just starting to brown in places. Return the pan to the oven and bake for another 5 to 10 minutes, until the crust is uniformly light golden brown. Let cool.

5. **To make the filling:** Scatter the pecans on a sheet pan and bake for about 7 minutes, until fragrant and light golden brown. Set aside to cool.

6. In a stand mixer (or with a hand mixer), beat together the brown sugar and corn syrup. Add the eggs and beat until thoroughly combined. Mix in the brandy, vanilla, and salt. Stir in the toasted pecans.

7. Pour the filling into the tart shell and bake for 20 to 25 minutes, until the center is slightly puffed and firm. Let cool before slicing and serving.

EVEN EASIER: Use refrigerated piecrust instead of making your own.

SIMPLE SWAP: Feel free to substitute bourbon or dark rum for the brandy, or leave the liquor out.

NUTMEG BUTTER COOKIES

VEGETARIAN | UNDER 30 MINUTES

For these cookies, be sure to use fresh nutmeg rather than the less flavorful pre-ground nutmeg (also see the Simple Swap tip).

MAKES 4 DOZEN

Prep Time: 10 minutes

Cook Time: 10 minutes

½ cup (1 stick) unsalted
  butter, melted

1 cup sugar

1 teaspoon vanilla extract

¼ teaspoon kosher salt

1 large egg

1 cup all-purpose flour

1½ teaspoons freshly
  grated nutmeg

1. Select Convection Bake and preheat the oven to 350°F. Line two sheet pans with silicone baking mats (or use one sheet pan and bake in batches).

2. In a large bowl, mix together the butter and sugar. Stir in the vanilla and salt. Add the egg and beat until the mixture is smooth.

3. In a small bowl, whisk together the flour and nutmeg. Stir the flour mixture into the sugar and butter mixture just until blended.

4. Drop the batter by level teaspoons onto the prepared pans, leaving about 2 inches around the dough balls.

5. Bake for 11 to 12 minutes, or until the cookies have spread, the edges are golden brown, and the tops start to collapse. Let cool on the pans for a few minutes, then transfer to a rack to cool completely.

FOR COUNTERTOP OVENS: Because these ovens hold only one smaller pan, you'll have to make the cookies in batches.

SIMPLE SWAP: If you don't have whole nutmegs to grate or just don't like nutmeg, you can use other spices, such as ground cinnamon. For an unusual twist, try ground cloves or five-spice powder, but with stronger flavors like these, reduce the amount to 1 teaspoon.

PEACH AND BLUEBERRY CRISP

VEGETARIAN | VEGAN OPTION

This recipe is easy and versatile, and it can be made ahead, refrigerated, and then baked—or made ahead, baked, refrigerated, and then warmed up for serving. Try topping the crisp with vanilla ice cream.

SERVES 4

Prep Time: 15 minutes

Cook Time: 30 minutes

FOR THE FILLING

Nonstick cooking spray

5 ripe yellow peaches

1 cup fresh or
    frozen blueberries

⅓ cup granulated sugar

1 tablespoon all-purpose flour

1 teaspoon grated lemon zest

FOR THE TOPPING

½ cup quick-cooking oatmeal

⅓ cup brown sugar

⅓ cup all-purpose flour

¼ cup blanched
    slivered almonds

1 teaspoon ground cinnamon

½ teaspoon ground cardamom

Pinch salt

4 tablespoons
    (½ stick) unsalted butter or
    vegan margarine

1. **To make the filling:** Select Convection Bake and preheat the oven to 350°F. Spray a 9-inch square baking pan with cooking spray.

2. Peel and pit the peaches. Slice them about ½-inch thick, then cut the slices in half. You should have about 4 cups of slices. Put them in a medium bowl and add the blueberries, sugar, flour, and lemon zest. Toss gently. Pour into the prepared baking pan.

3. **To make the topping:** For the topping, mix together the oatmeal, brown sugar, flour, almonds, cinnamon, cardamom, and salt. With a pastry cutter or a large fork, cut in the butter until the mixture is crumbly. (Or use a food processor, but don't overprocess.)

4. Sprinkle the topping over the fruit. Bake for 30 minutes, or until the top is lightly browned and the peaches are bubbling. Let cool for about 15 minutes before cutting. Serve warm.

SIMPLE SWAP: You can use any fruit you like in this crisp. If you use apples, slice them very thin, as they take a little longer to cook.

EVEN EASIER: Use sliced, frozen peaches. Thaw and drain thoroughly, then cut the slices into smaller chunks.

CANDY BAR COOKIE BARS

VEGETARIAN | UNDER 30 MINUTES

Peanuts, chocolate, and caramel make these chewy bars a delightful cross between a cookie and a candy bar. Sturdy enough for a lunchbox dessert, they also make great afternoon or evening snacks.

SERVES 4

Prep Time: 10 minutes

Cook Time: 20 minutes

¾ cup peanut butter

½ cup (1 stick) unsalted butter, softened

½ cup packed brown sugar

½ cup granulated sugar

1 large egg

1 teaspoon vanilla extract

1½ cups all-purpose flour

½ teaspoon baking soda

1½ cups bittersweet chocolate chips, divided

¾ cup salted roasted peanuts, very coarsely chopped

1 cup caramel sauce

1. Select Convection Bake and preheat the oven to 350°F.

2. Beat the peanut butter, butter, and sugars in a stand mixer (or with a hand mixer) until creamy. Beat in the egg and vanilla.

3. In a small bowl, whisk together the flour and baking soda, then gradually beat the flour mixture into the peanut butter mixture. Stir in half the chocolate chips, distributing them evenly in the dough. Press into a 9-by-13-inch baking pan.

4. Sprinkle the remaining chocolate chips and the peanuts over the dough.

5. Bake for 8 minutes, or just until the top of the dough is set, then remove the pan from the oven, drizzle with the caramel, and return to the oven for 10 to 12 minutes, until the caramel is bubbling. Cool completely, then cut into bars.

EVEN EASIER: To make these bars without the candy-like topping, skip the peanuts and caramel sauce, use crunchy peanut butter, and mix all the chocolate chips into the batter.

Cooking Charts

The following charts provide a starting point for cooking a variety of foods in standard and countertop convection ovens. In some cases, you can alter the method of cooking using a lower temperature and longer time (or higher temperature and shorter time), and, of course, you'll always want to check your food after about two-thirds of the time has passed to avoid overcooking.

MEAT

- When meats are cut into pieces, as for stews, the total weight is unimportant; what counts is the size of the pieces. Likewise, for steaks and chops, the thickness is the important factor, not the weight or number of pieces.

- Tender, lean cuts like fillet steaks or pork tenderloin do best with a higher temperature and shorter cooking period. Tougher cuts like pork or beef shoulder get best results with low temperatures and longer times.

- When cooking tougher cuts, cooking in liquid (as for stews) can benefit both the flavor and texture.

- Always salt meat ahead of cooking, up to an hour in advance.

FOOD	WEIGHT	CONVECTION FUNCTION	CONVECTION TEMPERATURE	COOKING TIME	DONENESS INDICATOR
Beef rib roast (prime rib), boneless	4 pounds	Roast	350°F	45 minutes to 1¼ hours	130°F (medium-rare) to 140°F (medium)
Beef tenderloin	1½ pounds	Roast	400°F	15 to 25 minutes	127°F (rare) to 140°F (medium)
Chuck roast, cut into chunks	N/A	Roast	300°F	1 to 1½ hours	
Chuck roast, for pot roast, 2 to 3 inches thick	2 pounds	Roast	300°F	1½ to 2 hours	Tender, juicy

FOOD	WEIGHT	CONVECTION FUNCTION	CONVECTION TEMPERATURE	COOKING TIME	DONENESS INDICATOR
Lamb loin chops, 1-inch thick	N/A	Roast	450°F	7 to 10 minutes	125°F (rare) to 140° F (medium)
Lamb stew meat (leg or shoulder)	N/A	Roast	300°F	1 to 1½ hours	Tender
Meatloaf	2 pounds	Bake	350°F	40 to 45 minutes	160°F
Pork shoulder, cut into chunks	N/A	Roast	300°F	45 to 60 minutes	Tender
Pork shoulder, roast	2 to 3 pounds	Roast	300°F	1 to 1½ hours	Tender, juicy
Pork tenderloin, cut into chunks	N/A	Roast	375°F	8 to 10 minutes	Barely pink inside
Pork tenderloin, whole	1 pound	Roast	375°F	20 to 25 minutes	145°F
Rack of lamb	1 pound	Roast	400°F	20 to 25 minutes	125°F (rare) to 140°F (medium)
Sirloin, flat iron steak, sliced	N/A	Roast	375°F	8 to 10 minutes	Slightly pink interior
Spareribs, rack	N/A	Roast	225°F	2 to 3 hours	Tender
Standing rib roast, bone-in	4 pounds	Roast	350°F	40 minutes to 1 hour	130°F (rare) to 140°F (medium)
Steaks (rib, strip, filet), 1½-inches thick	N/A	Broil	High	4 to 6 minutes per side	127°F (rare) to 140°F (medium)

POULTRY

- For juicier chicken and turkey breast, remove the meat from the oven when the internal temperature reaches 155°F. While it's true that the USDA recommends 165°F, that's the temperature at which pathogens are killed instantly. If your poultry stays at 155°F for 5 to 10 minutes (which it will), it will be safe.

- When deciding between chicken breasts and thighs for stews and braises, keep in mind that thighs will stand up better to long cooking, whereas breasts tend to dry out.

- For crisper chicken skin, salt ahead of time and dry thoroughly before cooking. A little baking powder mixed with the salt will aid in browning.

FOOD	WEIGHT	CONVECTION FUNCTION	CONVECTION TEMPERATURE	COOKING TIME	DONENESS INDICATOR
Chicken, whole	4 pounds	Roast	400°F	1 to 1¼ hours	155°F (breast), 170°F (thigh)
Chicken breast, boneless	8 to 10 ounces	Roast	375°F	15 to 20 minutes	155°F
Chicken breast, boneless, cut into chunks	N/A	Roast	375°F	8 to 10 minutes	Center opaque
Chicken legs/ thighs, bone-in	8 ounces	Roast	375°F	35 to 40 minutes	170°F
Chicken thighs, boneless	6 ounces	Roast	375°F	15 to 25 minutes	Center opaque
Duck breasts	8 ounces	Roast	350°F	1½ to 2 hours	140°F (rare) to 155°F (medium)
Turkey, whole	12 pounds	Roast	375°F	1¼ to 1¾ hours	155°F (breast), 170° F (thigh)

FOOD	WEIGHT	CONVECTION FUNCTION	CONVECTION TEMPERATURE	COOKING TIME	DONENESS INDICATOR
Turkey breast, bone-in	4 pounds	Roast	350°F	35 to 45 minutes	155°F
Turkey tenderloin, whole	20 pounds	Roast	375°F	20 to 30 minutes	155°F

SEAFOOD

- While the USDA recommends 145°F as the safe temperature for fish, many chefs prefer some fish, especially tuna and salmon, cooked to a lower temperature. America's Test Kitchen, for instance, calls for salmon to be cooked to 125°F.

- Since it can be difficult to get an accurate temperature reading on thin fillets, cooking fish until it flakes apart is a good way to ensure it's done.

- Because fish is comparatively lean, it's best to brush it with oil or butter before cooking, or cook with a sauce.

FOOD	WEIGHT	CONVECTION FUNCTION	CONVECTION TEMPERATURE	COOKING TIME	DONENESS INDICATOR
Cod fillet, 1-inch thick	N/A	Roast	400°F	1 to 1¼ hours	Opaque center, flakes apart
Halibut fillet, 1-inch thick	6 to 8 ounces	Roast	350°F	15 minutes	Opaque center, flakes apart
Salmon fillet, 1-inch thick	6 to 8 ounces	Roast	375°F	12 to 15 minutes	Opaque center, flakes apart
Salmon steak, 1-inch thick	8 ounces	Roast	375°F	12 to 15 minutes	Opaque center, flakes apart
Shrimp, large (21 to 26 per pound)	N/A	Roast	375°F	5 to 6 minutes	Opaque throughout
Snapper fillet, ¾-inch thick	8 ounces	Roast	425°F	15 to 20 minutes	Opaque center, flakes apart

FOOD	WEIGHT	CONVECTION FUNCTION	CONVECTION TEMPERATURE	COOKING TIME	DONENESS INDICATOR
Tilapia fillet, ¾-inch thick	8 ounces	Roast	350°F	12 to 15 minutes	Opaque center, flakes apart
Trout, whole, bone-in	1 pound	Roast	350°F	30 minutes	Flakes apart
Trout, whole, butterflied	10 ounces	Roast	400°F	20 to 25 minutes	Flakes apart
Trout fillet, ½-inch thick	5 ounces	Roast	350°F	15 to 18 minutes	Flakes apart
Tuna steak, ¾-inch thick	8 ounces	Broil	High	4 to 5 minutes per side	Pink center

VEGETABLES

- Always coat vegetables with oil or butter before roasting. The fat helps keep moisture in the vegetables, preventing them from drying out.

- Cut vegetables into consistently sized pieces so they cook evenly.

- In most cases, you should stir the vegetables once or twice during cooking. The vegetables at the outer edges of the pan will cook faster than those at the center, so move them around for even cooking.

FOOD	PREP	CONVECTION FUNCTION	CONVECTION TEMPERATURE	COOKING TIME	DONENESS INDICATOR
Asparagus, thick	Whole	Roast	375°F	12 to 15 minutes	Crisp exterior, tender
Asparagus, thin	Whole	Roast	375°F	10 to 13 minutes	Crisp exterior, tender

FOOD	PREP	CONVECTION FUNCTION	CONVECTION TEMPERATURE	COOKING TIME	DONENESS INDICATOR
Bell peppers	Cut into chunks	Roast	375°F	10 to 12 minutes	Crisp exterior, tender
Broccoli	Cut into florets	Roast	400°F	15 to 20 minutes	Tender
Brussels sprouts	Halved	Roast	400°F	18 to 22 minutes	Crisp exterior, tender
Carrots	1-inch pieces	Roast	425°F	20 to 25 minutes	Tender
Cauliflower	Whole	Roast	400°F	15 to 20 minutes	Crisp exterior, tender
Green beans	Whole	Roast	475°F	10 to 15 minutes	Crisp exterior, tender
Nuts, whole	Shelled	Bake	350°F	6 to 8 minutes	Golden brown and fragrant
Potatoes, baking	Whole	Bake	375°F	45 minutes to 1 hour	Knife inserts easily
Potatoes, baking (for oven fries)	½-inch sticks	Roast	425°F	35 to 40 minutes	Crisp, brown exterior
Potatoes, red	Halved if small, quartered if large	Roast	375°F	35 to 40 minutes	Crisp exterior, tender
Summer squash (zucchini, crookneck, etc.)	Sliced, salted	Broil	High	3 to 4 minutes per side	Lightly browned
Sweet potatoes	Whole	Bake	375°F	45 to 55 minutes	Knife inserts easily
Sweet potatoes (for oven fries)	½-inch sticks	Roast	400°F	35 to 40 minutes	Crisp, brown exterior
Winter squash (acorn, butternut, delicata, etc.)	Halved	Roast	400°F	40 to 50 minutes	Knife inserts easily

BAKED GOODS

- The ingredients in recipes for cakes, cookies, and other baked goods vary widely, which can affect the cooking times and temperatures. Always follow the recipe if it differs from this chart.

- When baking cookies for the first time, test one or two before baking a whole batch.

- Some baked goods, such as soufflés, are best baked without a convection fan. See page 10 for more information.

FOOD	CONVECTION FUNCTION	CONVECTION TEMPERATURE	COOKING TIME	DONENESS INDICATION
Biscuits	Bake	400°F	12 to 15 minutes	Golden brown and risen
Bread, standard loaf	Bake	350°F	30 to 60 minutes	Browned, hollow sounding
Brownies and bars	Bake	325°F	25 to 30 minutes	Toothpick comes out clean
Cake, Bundt	Bake	350°F	40 to 50 minutes	Toothpick comes out clean
Cake, layer	Bake	350°F	25 to 30 minutes	Toothpick comes out clean
Cake, pound	Bake	350°F	40 to 50 minutes	Toothpick comes out clean
Cookies	Bake	350°F	7 to 10 minutes	Varies
Cupcakes	Bake	350°F	18 to 20 minutes	Toothpick comes out clean
Fruit pie	Bake	350°F	40 to 50 minutes	Browned crust, bubbling filling
Muffins	Bake	350°F	25 to 30 minutes	Browned, puffed

FOOD	CONVECTION FUNCTION	CONVECTION TEMPERATURE	COOKING TIME	DONENESS INDICATOR
Pastry crust	Bake	400°F	20 to 30 minutes	Golden brown
Pizza	Roast	450°F	12 to 14 minutes	Browned
Quiche (par-baked crust)	Bake	400°F	17 to 20 minutes	Light golden brown, center set

Index

Acknowledgments

Thanks to the team at Callisto Media—Stacy Wagner-Kinnear, Wesley Chiu, and Van Van Cleave. Thanks also to Caitlin, Sean, and Dave for their help testing recipes. Special thanks to Mason for forgoing his video games while I worked on the manuscript.

About the Author

Janet A. Zimmerman is the author of seven other cookbooks, including the best-selling *Instant Pot Obsession*. She has received several food-writing awards, and her work has appeared in the annual anthology *Best Food Writing*. She and her partner, Dave, live in Atlanta.

Printed in the USA
CPSIA information can be obtained
at www.ICGtesting.com
CBHW082020220524
8972CB00005B/77